MW01234672

Selected titles from the YOURDON PRESS COMPUTING SERIES
Ed Yourdon, *Advisor*

The Information Asset

Rational DP Funding and Other Radical Notions

John Boddie

YOURDON PRESS
Prentice Hall Building
Englewood Cliffs, New Jersey 07632

Library of Congress Cataloging-in-Publication Data

Boddie, John
  The information asset : rational dp funding and other radical
  notions / John Boddie.
      p.   cm.
  Includes bibliographical references and index.
  ISBN 0-13-457326-9
  1. Industrial management--Data processing. 2. Management
  information systems. I. Title.
  HD30.2.B63   1993   92-38719
  658.4'038--dc20   CIP

Editorial/production supervision, interior
    design, page layout and
    interior illustrations: *Brendan M. Stewart*
Buyer: *Mary Elizabeth McCartney*
Acquisitions editor: *Paul Becker*

The publisher offers discounts on this book when ordered
in bulk quantities. For more information, contact:

> Corporate Sales Department
> PTR Prentice Hall
> 113 Sylvan Avenue
> Englewood Cliffs, New Jersey 07632
> Phone: 201-592-2863
> Fax: 201-592-2249

Printed in the United States of America
10 9 8 7 6 5 4 3 2 1

ISBN 0-13-457326-9

Prentice-Hall International (UK) Limited, *London*
Prentice-Hall of Australia Pty. Limited, *Sydney*
Prentice-Hall Canada Inc., *Toronto*
Prentice-Hall Hispanoamericana, S.A., *Mexico*
Prentice Hall of India Private Limited, *New Delhi*
Prentice-Hall of Japan, Inc., *Tokyo*
Simon & Schuster Asia Pte. Ltd., *Singapore*
Editora Prentice-Hall do Brasil, Ltda., *Rio de Janeiro*

Dedication

Almost unbelievably, my wife, Mardi, has again allowed me to commandeer a corner of the living room so that I could write. Both she and my children have been more than merely tolerant of the irritability which occasionally settles in during the writing process. It is because of this, and so many other and more important things, that this book is dedicated to her and to John, Katherine, and Andrew.

Contents

Preface

This book arose from my attempts to figure out what was going wrong. Many of my clients felt that they were losing control of the systems management process. They were being told that their systems did not do what the business needed. Requested improvements were often delayed or ignored. System costs were on an upward spiral, and it was difficult to relate these costs to tangible benefits. They feared that things weren't getting better.

The people who were making these complaints were not neophytes facing their first computer system. In many cases they were responsible for directing Data Processing activity in their firms. Many felt that their jobs were on the line.

Faced with this sense of uneasiness, we began to look at some of the underlying assumptions about Data Processing and the enterprise. We found several common beliefs that could not be squared with experience. Many of the issues seemed to be outside the area of Data Processing, but they appeared to be having a significant effect upon it. It became clear, as I discussed these issues with my clients, that we were considering making fundamental changes in the ways that the Data

Processing organization interacted with the other parts of the company; particularly in the area of obtaining funding for system development or modifications. We took some steps to begin these changes, and they are described in this book.

The jury is still out as to whether or not our insights will bring about all the changes we hoped for. As a consequence, this book should raise more questions than it answers. After considering the issues presented here you may reach conclusions which differ from ours. However, it is important that you recognize these issues and think about them in the context of your own experience. As one of my clients put it, "We've been making the same mistakes for fifteen years; at least this gives us the opportunity to make different ones."

This book is written for people who have management responsibility in Data Processing groups that serve business enterprises. I hope that it also proves useful to people in other parts of the business who use the services provided by Data Processing. It may seem unfair that I am laying the burden of responsibility for changing the relationship between Data Processing and the rest of the enterprise on the Data Processing group. The reason I do this is only because the changes are more easily initiated there.

The book consists of a series of essays that treat different aspects of a common theme - the need to change our Data Processing paradigm to focus on information rather than on data as well as the consequences of changing the paradigm. The chapters, for the most part, are short and can be read independently. The book starts by identifying characteristics of the current role of Data Processing in the enterprise and then examines some of the technical aspects of our work that affect the relationship between Data Processing and those who use its product.

The third part of the book focuses on some approaches to changing the paradigm. I do not believe there is a universal formula that can be applied in all cases. Enterprises are like living organisms and each has its own set of stimuli to which it responds. The value of the information asset shifts in response to events over which Data Processing will never be able to exert control. This should not worry us unduly. Sailors cannot control the sea, but they have learned how to sail from shore to shore. We should be able to do as well.

Notes on Terminology

There are many terms for the systems groups within an enterprise. Information Services, MIS, Information Systems, Information Management, Computer Technology—the list is extensive. Some enterprises have multiple groups, each with specific responsibilities. In this book, I have consistently used the term Data Processing, or DP, to refer to the group or set of groups that is responsible for managing computer activity in the enterprise. The reason I have focused on this outdated term should become clearer as you read the book.

The terms "enterprise" or "company" are used to refer to a business, governmental, or charitable organization that uses computers to manage data that is used on a regular basis during business operations.

His, her, she, him, and other indicators of gender are used throughout the book interchangeably. Until scientific data is presented proving otherwise, I will continue to believe that the chromosomes that determine sex are not the same ones that determine intelligence, energy, and the desire to do quality work.

In those places where I refer to executives, I mean to indicate that the people who hold these positions have some degree of policy-making responsibility. A company executive plays a role in establishing policies for the enterprise as a whole. A Data Processing executive has the responsibility for establishing policy within the Data Processing organization.

1-2-3 is a trademark of Lotus Development Corp., IBM is a trademark of International Business Machines, Inc.

Acknowledgments

Much of the material in this book appeared in its original form in Ed Yourdon's magazine, *American Programmer,* or in *Tech Exec,* which was the forerunner of *System 3x/400 Information Management.* I want to express my heartfelt thanks to Veronica Patterson and her staff at Duke Communications and to Ed Yourdon and Toni Nash at Children's Computer Company for the encouragement and opportunities they have provided me.

Many of the concepts presented here have been worked out in the course of consultation with clients and co-workers. The contributions of Erceal Doty and Lee Gantt of GTE, Frank Gargallo and Deborah Waggoner of TRECOM Business Systems, Joan Allessi of Simpatica, and Gloria Davis of GE Consulting have helped me greatly. My sincere thanks go to them and many others whose contributions are no less real or any less valuable for the absence of their names on this page.

It is an unfortunate characteristic of author's acknowledgments that they concentrate on people with whom the author has worked personally, giving little or no credit to other authors who have influenced the work at hand. I would like to say here that this book could never have come into being were it not for previous writing by Tom DeMarco, Tim Lister, John Palmer, Steve McMenamin, Ed Yourdon, Larry Constantine, Sherry Turkle, Barbara Bouldin, Gerald Weinberg, Frederick Brooks, Paul Ward, Arno Penzias, Raymond Smullyan, Robert Lucky, and others. In particular, by writing *In the Age of the Smart Machine,* Shoshana Zuboff has provided me with a means to clarify seemingly intractable issues, and I freely acknowledge my debt in this regard.

In addition to those who helped form the concepts presented in this book and those whose work fertilized the thought process, I would be remiss if I did not acknowledge those who actually performed the labor to turn the manuscript into a book. My editor, Paul Becker, has shown patience (far exceeding my own) in living with the delays that I have caused. Thank you, Paul.

1

The Great Divide

Virtually every business, government, or charitable enterprise relies on the use of information to achieve its goals. Many of these enterprises use computers to help them manage information. However, very few of these enterprises are in the computer business. This is often overlooked by those who tend the computers.

Many of the people responsible for providing computer services think of themselves as working in the Data Processing business. A steady stream of books, periodicals, and conferences reinforces this view by focusing on tools and techniques to be applied to the problems of using computer technology. The salaries and educational levels in the Data Processing business further feed the image of membership in an elite group. In addition, people who work in Data Processing organizations are familiar with equipment which has cost many millions of dollars and which is not readily understood by "non-computer people."

The language used in the Data Processing business reinforces the view that it is a self-contained world. It is generally easier for a programmer in one company to communicate with a programmer in another industry than it is for him to communicate with the sales manager in the firm that employs him. When the programmer speaks of improving his skills, he refers to programming skills that are valued by his peers within the Data Processing business.

It has become the rule rather than the exception that the Data Processing group has drifted apart from the enterprise it serves. The Data Processing organization has become separated by its concentration on technical skill, and by the honest belief that it is helping the enterprise by concentrating on what it does best.

This isolation of Data Processing should be a source of concern to companies that use computers, and it often is. Unfortunately, the concern is compounded by a feeling of helplessness. Companies have come to rely upon the computer in their day-to-day activities. Computers record orders, track shipments, monitor production, and maintain payroll records. The financial and operational consequences of disrupting Data Processing are taken very seriously by most company executives. The prevailing attitude seems to be that the problems with Data Processing are not so bad that they could not be made worse by an inept attempt to correct them.

This is not to say that the suffering is silent. Tales of systems that don't do what's needed, delays in building and delivering systems, and a seemingly insatiable appetite for larger budgets are all too common. In many firms, the computer has moved from its original position as "the solution" to a point where it is now "part of the problem." A 1989 survey by Coopers & Lybrand and *Datamation* magazine reveals that Data Processing: "…is not even viewed by the executive suite as a real profession. Instead, it is thought of as a poorly managed craft."

The real tragedy is that things may be getting worse.

The Mission

Most Data Processing managers would tell you, with all sincerity, that they regard service to the corporation as their mission. The mission is not going well. Computer systems analysts constantly decry the inability of the user to articulate his requirements. Users are regarded by Data Processing staff as being capricious and unreasonable, asking for changes that can involve massive system restructuring as if these changes could be accommodated in a day or two. The mutual frustration of users and Data Processing staff has all too often boiled over into personal acrimony. In response to perceived difficulties in dealing with users, many enterprises have set up internal units to insulate the people who build Data Processing systems from those who use them.

In all too many companies, Data Processing groups speak of "us" and "them" when talking about other parts of the enterprise. This is a poor foundation upon which to base a mission of service to the user.

> **Bernie Berlow, who numbers some excellently managed companies among his clients, gives an instructive example of the way that Data Processing can value service to the user. A middle-level manager for one of Bernie's clients needed a report that combined information he now had to retrieve from four different reports. The manager told Bernie that the Data Processing group had estimated that it would take three months to develop the new report.**
>
> **After about ten minutes of discussion Bernie and the manager had loaded some data from the mainframe into the manager's PC. Using a commercial report generator, it took them about twenty minutes more to set up the formats for the report the manager needed. Then they produced the report. Once this was done, they went to talk to the Director of Data Processing.**
>
> **The Director of Data Processing called in the analyst who had made the three month estimate. Bernie explained what he and the manager had done to get the report produced in half an hour. They told the analyst about the PC and the report generator package.**
>
> **The analyst was irate. "That's no good!" he said. "You cheated!"**

The perception that Data Processing is somehow independent of the enterprise of which it is a part is a very dangerous one. The data that is collected, organized, stored, and reported by computers becomes the information used by managers and employees of the enterprise. These people will use this information to make decisions that will affect jobs, production, and finances. If the data cannot be provided effectively, the quality of management and operations in the enterprise will suffer. The company may even fail.

There is no point belaboring the question of which side is at fault for the current state of affairs. The issue is to identify the practices which are driving Data Processing and the enterprise further apart, and to propose changes that will bring them back together.

This is easier said than done. Many practices within Data Processing organizations have been instituted to correct problems related to software quality and productivity. For a long time, programming was regarded as an art. Data Processing managers are still struggling with this heritage as they try to impose practices to make system development more like other forms of engineering—in a word, to make it more manageable.

The concentration on management *within* the data processing organization has led to neglect of the more important issue—that of management *of* the Data Processing function within the organization as a whole. Data Processing has become so concerned with the details of the cart that it has neglected the relationship with the horse.

The most straightforward way to bring Data Processing and the rest of the enterprise closer together is to bring the mission of Data Processing into sharper focus, both from an internal and an external perspective. It is very easy for Data Processing managers to say, "Service is our mission" and believe that service is being provided because users are getting something they did not have before. This is self-deception and it needs to be recognized as such.

The Challenge

Data Processing management needs to concentrate on answering two fundamental questions:

> **1.** What constitutes service to the user?
>
> **2.** How can performance in providing service to the user be measured?

Service to the user is defined by the user. Service, whether in data processing, law, medicine, or other human activity, is *always* defined by the party who receives the service. The surgeon may perform brilliantly, but if the patient dies, the value of the service, at least for the deceased, will not be counted highly.

In order to understand what service to the user is, the Data Processing staff must put aside their data processing knowledge and learn about the user's world. This does not happen often. Robert Townsend, in *Up the Organization,* described what happened when he put the head of Avis systems behind a rental counter to serve actual customers.[1] Clark Barlow, the Vice-president of GTE's Telephone Operations, insisted that all of the managers of his new Information Systems group go through a series of courses to learn the basics of the telephone business. The fact that such actions are thought of as unusual is a clear indication of the gulf between Data Processing and the rest of the enterprise.

The gulf is real, and it is often wide.

The user's world, like the world of data processing, has an extensive folklore. It may use its own terminology and do things that at face value seem inexplicable. The Data Processing staff may never understand the user's business as well as the user does, but they need to understand it at a level where they can communicate effectively. Without this effective communication, it will not be possible for the Data Processing staff to understand what the user means when he talks about the service he needs.

Unless the Data Processing group is able to understand what service is, they will not be able to provide it. There will simply be a continuation of the current ritual minuet where inappropriate systems are developed based on partial understanding, and users are forced to develop workarounds in order to carry out their assigned tasks.

As a consequence of the current way of doing things, many new systems are unveiled not to applause, but to a chorus of change requests. According to many Data Processing experts, the pressure for system modifications has produced a "maintenance crisis." It would probably be more accurate to refer to the "things that need to be done after the original system was delivered to improve its ability to serve the users" crisis.

For Data Processing to be effective, an understanding of what constitutes service to the user is not enough. Data Processing management also has a duty to track the level of service being provided. This may appear to be like wrestling with smoke since the definition of service is subject to change. Nevertheless, service must be measured if it is to be improved.

There is no shortage of Data Processing managers who claim that measuring service to the user in a meaningful way is impossible. This is not true. There is always a way of measuring something which is preferable to not measuring it at all.[2] Measure the cost to process an order, the number of user complaints, revenue per employee, or inventory levels. Pick something where the effects of the system can be seen. Internal measurements, such as system response time, are meaningless if the response doesn't contain the data the user needs.

1. The fellow fled at the approach of his first live customer.
2. This is known as *Gilb's Law* and is named for its formulator, Tom Gilb.

The technique of Function Point Analysis, which seeks to describe systems through the characteristics understood by users (screens, reports, files of data, etc.) is a hopeful first step in providing improved measurement. At present, the emphasis is on the use of this technique as a quantitative analysis tool. If qualitative considerations can be introduced in a consistent manner, Function Point Analysis could provide a significant advance in our ability to understand the systems we build.

Even with advanced tools at the disposal of the Data Processing group, the measurement of service must be worked out with the user, supported by the user, and applied consistently. In setting up a measure of user service, the Data Processing manager is bringing the mission of the Data Processing group out in the open where everyone can look at its performance.

It is very important that the measurement be kept publicly, and that it reflects the user's judgments. Otherwise the tendency of Data Processing to retreat into its technology-oriented shell will assert itself. The opportunity for real improvement will be lost. A regular program of measuring service to the user provides a mechanism where the Data Processing and user community managers will meet and work in concert on an issue of vital importance to the enterprise.

The existence of a public measure of service provides an anchor point for Data Processing activity. For every new project, every new tool, and every seminar attended, there should be a specific answer to the question, "How will this improve service to the user?" As a profession, Data Processing has drifted away from asking this question on a regular basis. It has concentrated on issues that are defined, evaluated, and resolved within Data Processing. An externally applied measure is required if this pattern of internal focus is to be broken.

The process of setting up a measure of user service is almost as important as the measure itself. It forces the Data Processing and user organizations to concentrate on an issue that joins them together as a unit. It breaks down the "us" and "them" mentality.

It is critical to break down this barrier if the further development and modification of systems is to be approached in a rational manner. The great divide between Data Processing and its users did not arise because either side wished for it to happen. Both parties concentrated on their appointed roles within the organization. They did so without realizing that they had a shared responsibility to the enterprise for the information asset that they jointly managed.

2

The Value of the System

The development, enhancement, and replacement of computer systems and software has been going on for over forty years. Systems have changed the way that business is done and, in some cases, have led to the creation of businesses that would not otherwise exist. Yet, with all the activity related to systems, it is a rare enterprise that attempts consistently to measure the value of the systems it uses.

The search for an answer to the question, "What is a system worth?" provides an excellent starting point in determining the contribution of the Data Processing function to the enterprise as a whole. It's a question that deserves a good answer.

The response to this question, like the answers to most questions, will reflect the interests of the people who are trying to supply an answer. The people who built the system will often take a technology-oriented approach and focus on the cost of hardware and on the cost to produce and install the programs. Sometimes they focus on the programs exclusively. The responses of users are usually less precise. They say things like, "I need these reports to track sales performance."

For all its imprecision, the response of the user points the way to a realistic measure of system value. The user is not thinking of the computers or of the programs that run in them. The manager in the sales department will talk about what she gets from the reports that come to her. She gets the information she needs to help her make decisions that will influence the success of the enterprise.

In the accounting department, the value of the system is reflected by what is *not* happening. There is no longer an army of typists preparing invoices and paychecks. The rows of desks where clerks entered transactions into ledgers have disappeared. The system has allowed the enterprise to lower its overhead costs.

For both the sales manager receiving her reports and the accounting department which no longer employs armies of people, the value of the system comes from what the system *does*, rather than from what it *is*. The focus is on outcome, not just output. The system has a role in the outcome because of its ability to retain data in an organized manner and to arrange and distribute the data to people who need it to do their jobs.

The data that has been collected and organized by computer systems is a store of value for the enterprise. Corporate information is as much of an asset as delivery trucks, office buildings, or patented processes. It yields a recurring benefit. Moreover, as with other assets, if no effort is made to keep the information asset in good condition, its value will erode.

Most company executives have no difficulty in recognizing that information is an asset. Despite this, most enterprises do not manage information from the point of view of increasing or preserving its asset value. Most enterprises haven't really thought about how to measure the value.

There is not very much material in Data Processing literature to help them. Barry Boehm in his classic book, *Software Engineering Economics,*[1] discusses the value of information in decision making related to software development activity, but provides little guidance in the determination of information value for the enterprise as a whole.

Daniel S. Appleton has published a number of articles[2] in *Datamation* and in other journals describing his company's "Information Asset Management" methodology. Unfortunately for the Data Processing manager who is

---

1. Barry W. Boehm, *Software Engineering Economics* (Prentice-Hall, 1981), Chapter 20.
2. Daniel S. Appleton, "Information Asset Management" in *Datamation*, 1 Feb 1986. Reprints of this and other articles related to Information Asset Management issues may be obtained from D. Appleton Company, Inc. 222 W. Las Colinas Blvd., Suite 1141, Irving, TX 75039

seeking guidance in this area, a comprehensive overview of his techniques is not available in book form. Mr. Appleton's articles do a good job of identifying the management issues associated with management of data and software assets, but they do not offer an approach to quantifying the asset value.

By far the best source of information in the existing literature is *Information Economics: Linking Business Performance to Information Technology* by Marilyn Parker and Robert Benson (Prentice-Hall, 1988). The authors use the measurement of *value* of information technology to the business performance of the enterprise as their fundamental theme. They discuss the need to coordinate actions in the "Business Domain" and "Technology Domain" in order to build value for the enterprise by obtaining advantages over the competition.

The material in Parker and Benson's *Information Economics* makes an excellent complement to the book you are now reading by providing extensive treatment of the classical project justification process. This book, *The Information Asset*, proposes a different manner of looking at the fundamental value of information in an enterprise. In this book, I will demonstrate that tying Data Processing activity to specific projects limits the ability of the enterprise to gain the maximum benefit from the information available for its use.

You should not be taken aback by the recommendation that you deal simultaneously with more than one point of view regarding the valuation of information and the treatment of associated funding issues. The nature of the information asset easily embraces multiple views of its characteristics and possibilities. These views can complement each other and you may need to use several of them as you work to convince others of the benefits that can be gained by changing current approaches to the planning and funding of Data Processing work.

A Different Kind of Asset

Information is a curious asset. It is unique in that it can be used by several different functional areas of the enterprise simultaneously. It's impossible to do this with fixed assets like forklift trucks. Information can be combined to create new assets without losing its identity. Depending upon where and how it is used, it can be worth a great deal or worth nothing at all.

The problems of measuring the value of the information asset are similar to the problems faced by the blind men when they examined the elephant. One man felt the leg and proclaimed that the elephant was like a tree, while another felt the tail and stated that the elephant was like a rope. The marketing department can look at account data and see it as the basis for decisions related to product promotions, while the shipping department sees it as a help in scheduling the company's trucks.

There is no universally recognized and easily applied formula to determine the value of data, although there is no shortage of promising and interesting approaches. For example, it seems reasonable to postulate that the value of data is determined by the context of its use—allowing a form of market valuation that could be further investigated using the tools of game theory. In fact, a substantial body of academic research has been performed on the impact of information differentials in game situations.

From a completely different quarter, Chris Meyer of Mercer Management Consulting has proposed a fascinating concept: that of examining information value using the principles of thermodynamics. Thermodynamics teaches us that differences in levels of entropy are the conditions that allow work to be performed. In information terms, if I have data that my competition doesn't have, I can increase my position in the market and I can continue to do this until I no longer enjoy a marked information superiority.

For the intellectually curious such approaches are a fertile ground for creative ideas. Unfortunately, the sad fact is that these approaches, rooted in sophisticated mathematics and scientific method, are not practical in the world of business. Applying them is complex and determining value is time-consuming. Furthermore, the answers produced will probably need to be translated into a form that can be readily understood by those who will pass on Data Processing funding.

It is the need to provide an understandable, defendable value for the information asset that has led to the approach presented in this book. The approach is not a panacea. It is not always easy to apply. It will not suddenly bring total rationality to the funding process. It does, however, have the advantage that you can learn a great deal about your business from both the exercise and the results. This alone should give you a better perspective on Data Processing investment as well as help you to improve Data Processing's contribution to the enterprise as a whole.

Before we consider the process of determining value, we might want to think about what we will do with the answer. If we say that information is an asset, how do we go about managing it as one? All too often we talk about the assets of an enterprise and make little effort to differentiate the tangible ones from the intangible. Data is certainly tangible. Consider whether it can be managed following the path of a traditional asset life cycle, as shown in Figure 2-1.

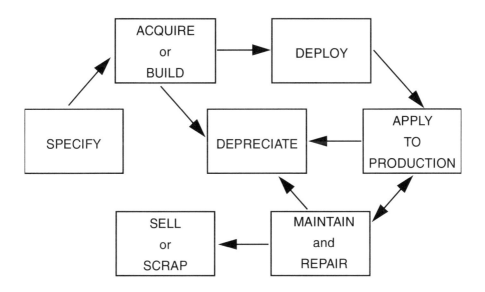

Figure 2-1 The Life Cycle of a Tangible Asset

Attempts to use this model to describe the way that data is managed fall short because they fail to capture the dynamic nature of data use. What seems more reasonable is a life cycle representation like the one shown in Figure 2-2.

In managing other tangible assets, we attempt to maximize their application over their useful life. In managing the information asset, we don't have the luxury of depreciation schedules based on physical phenomena. The concept of "useful life" is difficult to apply. Instead, we will take the approach that management of the information asset focuses on maintaining or increasing the recurring economic benefit derived from the data that we have collected, organized and put to use.

Applying the Scale

Even before computers came on the scene, the primary benefit of collecting, organizing, storing and using data was the proven ability of information to improve production, service and management processes. In ancient Egypt records were kept of agricultural production. This data was used to evaluate the performance of the Pharaoh's overseers. By ensuring that the Pharaoh was served by an effective staff, the production process was improved.

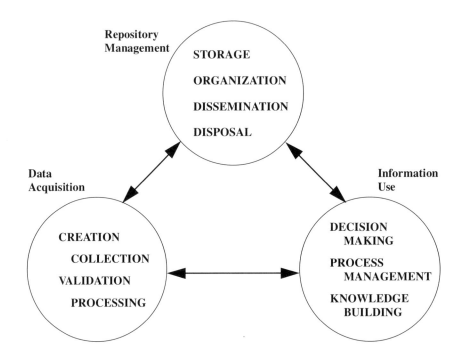

Figure 2-2 The Data/Information Asset Life Cycle

The improvement of a process yields a recurring benefit. If you can reduce the cost of processing an order from \$1.00 to 60¢, you will save 40¢ on each order you process, year after year. A measure of process improvement of particular interest is "cost of quality." This term was coined by Philip Crosby. Mr. Crosby is a respected authority on quality in the workplace and is the author of *Quality is Free*[3] and other books on the subject.

The cost of quality reflects the common-sense notion that the enterprise must invest resources in order to achieve the level of quality it desires. The cost of quality is directly related to the costs of error, waste, and delay —costs that process improvement will reduce. Process improvement is

3. Philip B. Crosby, *Quality is Free* (McGraw-Hill, New York, 1979). Crosby's other books on quality and management include *Quality Without Tears* and *Running Things: The Art of Making Things Happen.* As you read *Quality is Free*, you're sure to notice several parallels between the challenges facing information asset approaches and those facing the introduction of effective quality programs.

achieved when quality levels are maintained at a lower cost or if quality is raised by a factor which exceeds the resource investment.

The chances are pretty good that your organization already has data that can be used to measure improvements in cost of quality. When this data is correctly organized and applied, your organization can identify and reduce prevention, appraisal and failure costs. As these costs of quality are methodically reduced, the fundamental business processes are improved. This improvement allows the resources of the enterprise to be focused on today's business rather than on yesterday's mistakes.

The cost of quality can be reduced by finding ways to perform work effectively with fewer people. Reduction of the labor cost per successful unit of production or service is a classic measure of process improvement. If there were twelve people tracking inventory and coordinating replacement orders, and the introduction of a computer-supported system now allows the work to be done by three people, it's reasonable to conclude that the process has been improved and that the data managed by the system was responsible for the decrease.

When measuring labor savings, do not forget to make allowances for growth in the volume of activity. If twelve people handled 70,000 orders per year and now three people process 120,000, a straightforward calculation will show that the system has contributed to saving the equivalent of seventeen positions, not just nine.

What is being measured in this way is a proven reduction in cost per unit. Some managers may be uncomfortable with the extrapolation of labor savings to correspond to increased volumes of business, thinking it is an accounting trick. After all, they reason, seventeen positions weren't eliminated, only nine. Such concern is not justified. Virtually any aid to productivity derives some of its value through cost avoidance. Machines can do some things better than people can, and we need to recognize this fact and use it in assigning value to the machines.

In some cases information systems have allowed companies to provide new services that never had a parallel in manual operations. How can the cost of quality differentials be calculated in these cases? It's more straightforward than it seems initially. Modern structured analysis techniques require that the functionality of the system be determined before the processors are selected. Working from a model of the overall business process, a good analyst should be able to break down the work into discrete processes that can be handled by human "processors." Once this is done, it's a straightforward matter to count the number of people (processors) involved.

Some aspects of process improvement through labor savings are more difficult to deal with, such as extrapolating all the costs of a larger staff. You would need to calculate the costs of:

- •A larger facility
- •More work for payroll and personnel departments, which would have to grow as well
- •More internal communications and probably more middle management
- •The administrative staff additions needed for the larger workforce

rather than trying to factor all of these variables into the cost of quality equation, it would be better to use the current burdened cost values employed by your financial managers.

Using the current burdened cost will leave the estimates for cost of quality improvement on the conservative side, but there is no harm in doing that. Using cost factors provided by the company's financial people is a good way of involving them in the asset valuation process, and it is in the interest of the enterprise to see this done.

It does very little good for the Data Processing group to announce that the data in the company's systems is worth two billion dollars. It might well be worth that, but corporate executives may regard such a valuation as being a self-serving move on the part of the systems people. The executives may feel that systems people lack the expertise to accurately determine what the value is.

Value assessments coming from the finance department are a different story. If the Chief Financial Officer tells the other executives that the company's data is worth two billion dollars, the consequence is likely to be a sudden increase in attention paid to the Data Processing function.

It is generally not difficult to obtain assistance from the finance group. In most cases a direct approach and an explanation of what the Data Processing group is trying to do will gain a cooperative response. If the finance group has a problem in freeing up resources, you should explain that you need to establish the value of the information as a basis for evaluating the many requests for systems development and enhancement. Both Data Processing and finance managers need a way to cut through the competing claims for minimum cost/maximum benefit; claims which are routinely put forward by anyone who wants some systems work done.

Some companies are now using measures such as increase in shareholder value and EVA (Economic Value Added) as standard metrics for financial performance. These can operate to your advantage. Efforts to place a clear and understandable monetary value on the information asset can help in the task of determining the true economic performance of the enterprise.

Direct labor savings is only one of the outcomes of process improvement through improved data collection and distribution. Another is improved equipment utilization. Better record keeping means that the company can keep more of its plant and equipment busy by knowing what is available for immediate use.

There is also a benefit derived from inventory reduction. By knowing quantities and demand, and matching this information with production schedules and supplier lead times, the stock of both materials and finished goods can be scaled more accurately to the needs of the company. Furthermore, the improved ability to project inventory movements can free financial resources. These resources can then be invested to generate additional revenue.

How do we measure these benefits? The best place to start is by asking the finance department how they measure the effects. Just as with direct labor savings, you should be able to compile a set of "how it is now" and "how it was then" values. When the compilation is completed, the easiest thing to do is to propose a flat percentage to be assigned to the difference between these two values. The flat percentage chosen should reflect more than a token contribution for the Data Processing aspects of process improvement. Improvements in manufacturing techniques will account for some improvement in the reduction of inventory, but improved techniques must share credit for improvement with the changes in work organization and support enabled by better information management.

While calculating the value contributed by the information to savings of this sort, be careful not to count the direct manpower effects more than once. You are not trying to build an internal sales document by inflating numbers, you are trying to set up a solid base for systems planning over the long term.

In many cases the presence of organized data makes it possible to improve quality while reducing other costs. The cost of quality should decline as processes and personnel skills improve. It is no accident that the Baldridge Award process places considerable emphasis on the manner in which an enterprise collects, manages, and uses the data at its disposal.

After you have quantified the benefits the company gets from its Data Processing systems, go back and take out the costs associated with computer operations, personnel, and equipment. You don't need to calculate a net benefit in order to determine the asset value of the company's information, but you should be prepared to develop some return on investment values.

Identify not only the recurring benefits (process improvement this year should extend to next year as well), but the trends related to them. Is business volume rising at a faster rate than head count? How fast are wages growing? What are the cost trends for equipment that was recovered? This will give you both past, present, and future benefits. It will allow you to project the information asset value and establish a standard for future reference.

Once you have identified the recurring benefits, use the current rate of interest paid on a Certificate of Deposit to calculate how much the company would need to invest in order to get the same recurring benefit from another source. The result of the calculation is the asset value of the information.

If the recurring benefit is $650,000 a year and CD's are paying 9.5 percent, the value of the asset is over $6,800,000. For really large companies and systems, the numbers may be breathtaking. One database used by a major telecommunications company has been calculated to have an asset value of over four billion dollars.

Whether it's $6.8 million or $4 billion, the asset value of the information is something that can be counted on to attract notice from company executives. It is a representation of what the information means to the business, and it is presented using a standard yardstick—money.

Acceptance of the asset value as a measure of system contribution to the enterprise provides a base for changing the way that systems are planned and managed. It provides a solid foundation for initiatives to increase the use of current information, and provides a spur to actions which can strengthen the company's information infrastructure.

Most importantly, it finally brings the Data Processing group into the mainstream of the enterprise. The outcomes of data processing activity can be expressed in the common language of financial contribution to the enterprise. The linkage between the Data Processing group's activities and the activities of other groups within the enterprise can be made clearer.

Reinvesting in the Asset

A major benefit of asset-based systems planning is that such planning can provide some discretionary funding to underwrite the strategic maintenance of systems and data—the infrastructure of the information asset. Compared to broad-based maintenance programs for other assets of the enterprise, ongoing preventive maintenance in Data Processing has a very narrow focus. It is concerned almost entirely with the computer equipment. Software maintenance is, for the most part, reactive rather than proactive.

The first reinvestment should always be in the area of measurement. The establishment of a systems quality and effectiveness measurement program is a necessary first step in safeguarding the value of the information asset. Techniques such as statistical quality control of data and software development are well-documented,[4] and they are becoming increasingly important as systems move from centralized processing to distributed processing.

Activities that protect and enhance the value of the information asset tend to be long-term, requiring a consistent level of commitment and attention. A regular program of data access analysis is hardly the stuff which would win a Nobel Prize in software, assuming there were such a thing. However, changes in access patterns can be a useful signal that certain data is becoming obsolete, inaccurate, or irrelevant.

By paying attention to the findings in the strategic maintenance process, the Data Processing organization can take the steps necessary to adapt to changing business needs and do so in a smooth and controlled manner. This, in itself, may lead to faster response at lower cost—the sort of result which has a direct and immediate effect on the cost of quality.

Discretionary funds may be used also to increase the skill level of the Data Processing staff, by exposing programmers, analysts and managers to new tools, techniques and methodologies. It is foolish to think that we now stand at the apogee of computing technology, or that recent developments are largely irrelevant.

User education must not be left out of the re-investment program. An organized effort should be made to educate users about the capacities and possibilities of the Data Processing organization and the sources of data that are available both inside and outside the enterprise. The value of the information asset comes through its use and the Data Processing group should take the lead in extending this value.

---

4. The best treatment to date of this subject is by John D. Musa, Anthony Iannino, and Kazuhira Okumoto of Bell Laboratories in their book *Software Reliability: Measurement, Prediction, Application* (McGraw-Hill, 1987).

3

Determining Asset Value: A Practitioner's Approach

The job of assigning a realistic, understandable, and defendable value to the data which is administered by the Data Processing group involves considerable detective work. And, just as in the legal system, sloppy detective work can make it difficult to present one's case.

The first thing to remember is that the basis for provable value of most Data Processing activity is demonstrated process improvement—specifically improvements in the cost of quality. This does not mean that all value comes from cost-related factors. It means that comparisons between business activity where data is managed by the computers and similar business activity unsupported by computer based Data Processing provide the basis for effective presentations of the value which Data Processing has brought to the enterprise.

A second source of value comes in the form of revenue enhancement. In certain classes of systems, such as financial systems, the additional revenue obtained through the improved management of data can be measured using readily available account data. Other revenue enhancements may be indirect, such as improved sales performance resulting from improved use of customer information. In situations where the value of the information asset is realized indirectly, the task of quantifying it and establishing it as a basis for future decision making can be difficult. There may be general agreement that value is present, but the task of quantifying it will be subjective and, accordingly, the assessed value may be difficult to defend.

Data has always been used in the enterprise, but not always in a controlled, consistent manner. In the early days of the telephone company, the information needed to make a connection between the calling and called parties resided, for the most part, in the accumulated knowledge of local telephone operators. You have probably seen photographs of rows of ladies sitting at switchboards with a garden of plugs and cables in front of them. It was the operator's knowledge of the customers and numbers in the community that led to the rapid connections which telephone users came to expect. In today's telephone companies, the rows of local operators are long since gone, but the same type of information they used is still present. For the person who must put a value on the systems which now do the work of the operators, there needs to be a consistent way of expressing the economic value of this change.

A Simplified Example

Before we get into a detailed example of the way in which the value of data is determined, a simpler example may help to present the overall approach.

When I started renting cars from Hertz, I had to do a number of things when I came to the rental counter. I had to provide my driver's license and credit card and then wait while the agent keyed a lengthy set of information about me, the car, and the rental rate (plus discounts) into the computer. This information was then printed onto an involved paper form. If I needed directions, the agent and I consulted a map and traced out a route on a map copy that I took with me.

Today most of the information about me is kept with my Hertz #1 Club membership account. I still have to show my license and credit card and select a car, but the amount of information that the operator enters on the screen has been reduced by almost 90 percent. The form doesn't take nearly as long to print either. If I need directions, I step up to a special-purpose computer, select my destination, and receive a printed set of driving instructions.

The effect of these changes is that the Hertz agent now spends less time in performing the actions needed to get me into my car. The business consequences are that I can get better service (I'm driving off the lot in my rental car faster than I used to) while, at the same time, Hertz needs fewer agents. Since the service is just as good as it used to be (sometimes it's better), we are probably accurate in concluding that Hertz has improved its rental counter process and lowered its cost of quality.

Two factors here can be claimed as elements in the value provided by Data Processing. The first is the process improvement made possible by reducing the time required for an agent to interact with a customer in setting up the rental agreement. As was just pointed out, this translates to fewer agents. If Data Processing were not available, the job could still be done, but it would take more people and larger working facilities to do it. The difference between the time spent with and without Data Processing is a measure of the level of process improvement. It can be quantified, explained, defended, and extrapolated.

The second measure is increased customer satisfaction through the reduction of delays. This leads to increased customer loyalty and additional new customers persuaded by word of mouth to use Hertz. It is an increase in quality. There is no question that Data Processing made a contribution in this area, but the quality improvement will be more difficult to quantify, explain, defend, or extrapolate than the effect on the size of the workforce. As a result the value assigned to this measure is likely to be relatively small, although the contribution to perceived quality may be much higher.

Once we are able to determine some values for the first and second measures, we can then deduct the cost of system development and operation. This determines the net value to Hertz for having this system, and therefore the asset value of the data which the system manages.

Although this is a somewhat simplified approach (Hertz can also use the rental data to develop customer profiles, plan fleet sizes, identify automobile model preferences and other things) it does illustrate the basic method which should be followed.

A Case Study in Asset Value Determination

The more detailed example, which makes up the heart of this chapter, is related to a specialized equipment management system used by telephone companies. The incentive to determine the asset value of the data was an attempt to change the funding basis for system enhancements. The Data Processing manager responsible for the system felt that the funding basis in place at that time was biased toward approval of short-term, piecemeal enhancements. He believed such enhancements reduced the overall architectural integrity of the system. He felt that determination of the asset value could be used as an argument to establish on-going funding for a set of system restructuring activities. We all thought it would be a straightforward job.

At the most basic level telephone companies do two things; they arrange equipment to provide network access to the customer, and they charge the customer for using the equipment. The data describing the way in which the network equipment is arranged is used to support practices which touch many areas of the telephone company's day to day operations, such as the way your order for call-waiting is handled. The equipment management system is used to maintain the records that describe equipment arrangement and usage. It also provides access to that data for several other systems. The system being examined had several thousand users—a testimony to the usefulness of the data.

Because the role of the system was generally understood in the company, we felt that a quick analysis effort would identify the areas where the system provided benefits. What happened, in fact, was that the analysis became a lengthy, involved process—one which generated several sharp disagreements on many points of detail among the analysts and between the analysts and the system's users.

The most difficult part of determining the asset value of the enterprise's information turned out to be the initial data gathering. There were several times which we thought to ourselves, "There *must* be an easier way to do this." Having concluded the exercise and others very much like it, I have concluded that there isn't an easier way. However, those of us who worked on the project found that we came away with an in-depth understanding of the relationship between Data Processing activities and the work practices of the people who used the data.

The approach that we selected for determining value based on process improvement was to trace the increases in productivity for the job functions that were clearly affected by the equipment management system. This approach had been used for several years to determine the value of changes in work practices. Its heritage reaches back to the introduction of time and motion studies in the workplace.

We identified thirty-one business processes that used the telephone equipment data. From these, we selected seven in which this data played a key role. The selection process was guided by the time and manpower available to complete the study, and by our belief that the value of the data could best be demonstrated by using a few good examples.

We started by looking at financial data related to the cost of operations. The company retained budget and financial reports showing planned and actual expenditures for different operational units for many years. We obtained the manpower and salary amounts by job classification from records kept by the personnel department. We encountered little difficulty in obtaining an extensive set of documents and statistics, but we encountered considerable difficulty in understanding them.

One of the job functions that we wanted to track was that of Central Office Assignment. There is a lot of equipment in the telephone company's central offices—the places where the actual telephone switches which connect calls to and from your telephone are located. The wires that come from your home or office are connected to other wires in the increasingly large cables which run into the central offices. The central offices use other cables, called "trunks," to carry communications to other central offices. When you order telephone service it's necessary for someone inside the central office to make a connection between the wires coming into the central office from your home or business to the specialized equipment located in the central office that can connect you to the places you want to call. The job of selecting the equipment in the central office which will be used complete the circuit that provides your telephone service is Central Office Assignment.

Prior to the introduction of computers, records tracking the identification and use of central office equipment were kept in "cable books" and were updated by hand. A Central Office Assigner would look up the record for the cable which would carry your connection into the central office, and then would look at other records to identify unused locations on the wiring frames that could provide the services you ordered. A selection was made, the entries in the cable book were updated, and an order was written instructing a technician to connect the correct jumper wires from the cable to a point on the connecting frame. The procedure was reversed if you were having your service disconnected, but in this case, another connection had to be made to an operator or a recorded message that told callers that your number was no longer in service.

Problems in Obtaining Historical Data

When we started looking for data describing the expense for Central Office Assignment, we found that there had been several reorganizations and changes in job classifications over the period we were studying. There was no consistent single entry that said "Central Office Assignment." It became necessary to review job classifications in detail and interview employees who had held these assignments in order to develop a process history for the Central Office Assignment function. The process history we developed traced the cost and productivity of Central Office Assignment for over fifteen years.

During the course of our interviews we found that the introduction of improved central office equipment had led to changes in operating practices. The introduction of new wiring frames changed the layout of the central office, and led to different work requirements in connecting specialized components to the circuits. In some cases this increased the time required to perform the assignment, and in other cases it reduced it. This meant that in order to develop an accurate process history, we needed to relate work patterns to the type of service orders that were handled by the central office.

Talk about a can of worms—it seemed that every time we identified a factor that would help us determine the unit cost of Central Office Assignment prior to Data Processing, we found that there were two additional factors that also had to be accounted for. Our attempt to gather information was growing unmanageable.

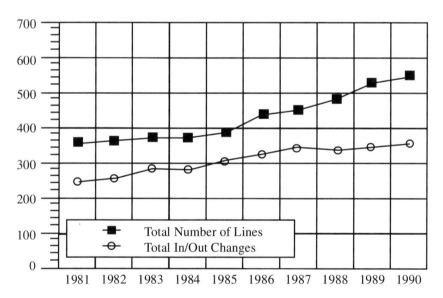

Figure 3-1 Underlying Business Activity

The first task was to obtain indicators of business activity that directly affected Central Office Assignment. These were the total number of lines installed by the telephone company that could be used for customer access, and the number of actual changes (putting lines in service or out of service).

We were fortunate in having good local records for a few of the operating divisions. This enabled us to develop a useful set of control values that could be applied as sanity checks to those estimates we received from areas where detailed records had not been as scrupulously maintained.

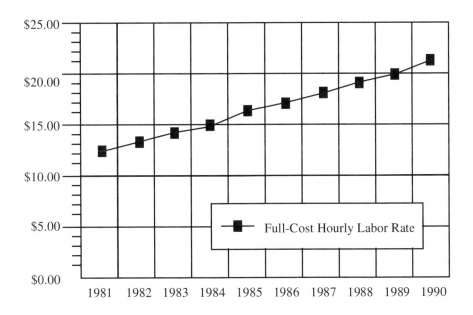

Figure 3-2 Hourly Labor Rates

This is more foundation material. The labor rates are important because an hour saved year-to-year increases in value as the labor rates go up. We did not feel it was necessary to adjust for constant 1980 dollars in the study.

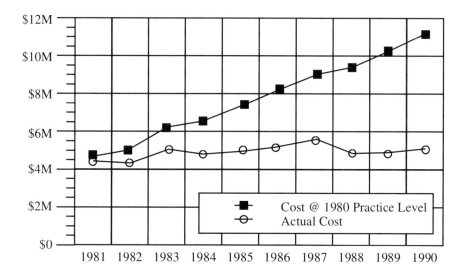

Figure 3-3 Cost Comparison

This is the comparison of the business activity costs, projected by using the productivity levels prior to the introduction of automation and the actual costs for Central Office Assignment. The area between the two lines is the savings realized from process improvement.

Detailed records about the cost of operations were difficult to find for the majority of the operating units. This, more than any other factor, increased the time and difficulty of the analysis. The age of the system that we were evaluating worked against us. It meant that in some cases we needed to gather data that was over ten years old in order to establish our baseline.

Because of the significant shift in Data Processing capabilities in recent years the temptation will be strong to simply determine the incremental increase in information asset value associated with the shift. This may be a straightforward task because some of the data may be present in existing data archives. Such information does have value, and it may be a good idea to use it to support limited objectives, such as obtaining funding for a desired system enhancement.

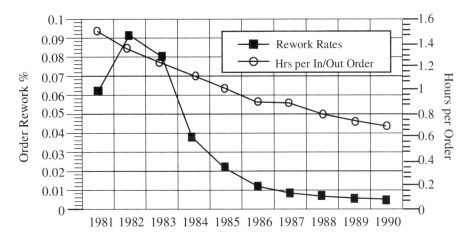

Figure 3-4 Quality Indicators

This is the rate of process improvement as measured by the decline in the hours per unit worked. Also shown is the Rework Rate for In and Out Orders that were incorrectly executed. The decline in rework is directly correlated to a reduced cost of quality.

In many cases you may find that this is the only option open to you because of gaps in the historical data. Situations involving company reorganizations, mergers, or radical shifts in process technology are extremely difficult to analyze—especially for the purposes of establishing a base for process improvement measurement. You may decide that the additional effort required for a complete historical baseline is simply not worth the research effort. The time pressure associated with the budget process may help you in reaching this decision.

If possible you should persevere in establishing a full set of historical data. Determination of incremental value based on recent system changes cannot provide the base you need to fully understand the asset value of the data managed by the Data Processing operation. As a general rule newer computer systems build on a base of data managed by the systems that preceded them. The true value of the data cannot be determined by examining the effects of the most recent system upgrade, any more than the true strength of the enterprise can be gauged by reading the most recent annual report.

What needs to be remembered is that systems and data provide value only to the extent that they support changed work practices and improve the overall business process. In order to establish the full degree to which they provide value it is necessary to compare those practices that are supported by the computer with practices that are not. Such measurements are effectively immune from obsolescence because the base value is not sensitive to current or future levels of technology.

The approach of starting from manual practices to determine a base for valuation introduces a bias you should be aware of. When automation is introduced in the workplace it is initially applied to one set of work practices and then, later, to another set. You need to keep in mind that changes which automate one set of practices may also cause changes and raise productivity in related but non-automated practices.

Let us say that we are measuring productivity in two work processes, A and B. We find that the introduction of automation in process A raised productivity in process B by fifteen percent. We also find that after introducing automation to process B directly, productivity in process B has increased by sixty percent when compared to the pre-automation level. We need to recognize that the introduction of automation to work process B yielded a productivity gain of forty-five percent, not sixty percent.

In the telephone equipment management system described in this chapter, there is a great deal of data related to the "outside plant"—equipment such as the cables that connect the telephone company central office to the junction boxes and the smaller cables which come to our homes and offices. This data was still handled manually in the cable books for several years after the central office records were computerized. The practices for some of the people who handled the outside plant had already been affected by the computerization of central office data. Assessing the cost for outside plant practices from a point before any telephone equipment data was stored on computers introduces a bias that overstates the process improvement. By the time that the outside plant data was handled by computer, benefits had already been realized as a by-product of central office automation.

Although we recognized this problem we did very little about it, with the exception of using some "best guess fudge factors" to account for benefits already realized. We used the fudge factors only to ensure that we would have a response if our valuation exercise was challenged. As it turned out, nobody considered the need to account for previously realized savings to be very important. The major concern was for the total value of the process improvement, not assignment to the component parts that made the savings possible.

The lack of concern as to the relative contributions of two different areas of functionality resulted from the fact that both functions (central office and outside plant) were supported by a single family of systems. I doubt that our task in this area would have been as easy if we were trying to assess the asset value for a set of data or systems that were used in coordination with other sets of systems in supporting a complex business process. If that had been the case, there would have been pressure to assign asset value to each system and then to determine the degree to which the asset value resulted from the manner in which the systems worked in concert.

Assignment of value in families of systems should be done by establishing the ownership share of the data by the various business processes which create and modify it. First the business processes that use the data are identified. Next, the increases in productivity related to the introduction of automated support are documented using the methods described for Central Office Assignment. Specific improvements which can be directly tied to the introduction or improved use of specific data are quantified and summed to establish a minimum provable contribution.

In those situations where a number of automated support functions have been introduced to a business process simultaneously or in rapid succession, an assessment of their individual contributions requires an "objectively subjective" judgement. If support function A is used to handle all customer inquiries, and support function B is called into play only for those inquiries involving past-due balances, then the contribution of function A to the improvement in productivity of the customer service group can be expected to be greater than that of function B. This can be verified by establishing the percentage of inquires where past-due balances are involved, and by establishing the times required to respond to these inquires before and after automated support was introduced.

A lot of fine-grained fact gathering and analysis is required to correctly establish the value that Data Processing has brought to the business functions it serves. The analysis is not high-tech or glamorous. But it's the only way to know—to really understand—the impact and value of the data managed by the enterprise's computer systems.

For an organization which has adopted a measurement system which tracks improvements in business quality and productivity, research to determine the labor savings resulting from the introduction of computer systems should be straightforward. Unfortunately, very few enterprises have taken the trouble to adopt or consistently use such measuring systems. For most of us, developing the baseline data will involve a lot of digging and interpretation.

Value Through Improved Inventory Management

Another important area where process improvement is realized is in the management of physical assets held in inventory. In the telephone company, improved information about equipment "in use," "available" or "defective," translated into a greater utilization factor than was achieved with manual records. An example of a utilization factor is that of cable pairs. Each pair of wires in a cable can be used to make up an individual telephone circuit. The utilization factor for a cable with one hundred pairs is the number of non-defective pairs that are actually in use. If there are ninety pairs in use, the utilization factor is ninety percent.

Before the records were computerized (telephone companies use the term, "mechanization") usage records were subject to errors associated with manual record keeping. What happened is that the cable book could show a utilization factor of ninety percent, where it might be actually seventy-five percent. Even worse, there was no economical way of checking the accuracy of the records.

This translated to higher costs for the telephone company. The number of cables which had to be installed was fifteen percent more than the number really needed (90% - 75%). The cost of designing and installing a cable is substantial, and installing fifteen percent more cables than necessary translates to many millions of dollars.

We were fortunate in finding several operating units within the company where managers had maintained detailed records of utilization factors in order to evaluate their unit's performance and efficiency. Utilization factors showed an increase which could accurately be correlated with the implementation of the equipment management system. It looked like this part of calculating the cost avoidance would be straightforward.

Actually it almost was. The only significant problem was the perceived need to provide a weighting for the two elements which the operating units felt contributed most to the improved utilization factor. The first element was the work done cleaning up the cable book information prior to entering it in the computer. The second element was the actual improvement in performance gained by using the improved information.

Judgments of this type are subjective. It was recognized that the efforts that improved the accuracy of the data were the primary source of savings. Lousy data in a computer system won't help anyone make better decisions than they would if the lousy data was on paper. What the computer system did was to help keep new errors from finding their way into the data.

The improvement in data quality was the result of a manual operation by the operations staff. They traced cable leads and made tests on cable pairs that were listed as defective. The operations group felt that they should receive credit for this work and that the value should not be assigned to the computer system. The systems people took the approach that it was the introduction of the system that provided the impetus for the data quality improvement effort. They also pointed to the fact that the presence of the system was keeping the records at an accurate level, and was a prime contributor to keeping the utilization factor high.

In the end we compromised. The operations group took half the credit and the systems people took the other half. The manner in which value is assigned is an important point which you should remember when you are attempting to determine the value of your data. It is not enough to have a quantified value which you believe in. It is equally important that other parts of the organization become attuned to the fact that the data in the computers represents an asset of considerable value to the enterprise. The extent to which they feel an ownership stake in that asset will make it easier to change the basis for funding data processing activity in the future.

Analysis of the benefits of improved data use in managing inventory will become more important as companies move toward partnership relationships that break down some of the barriers inherent in the old customer/vendor model of business. Wal-Mart has established a series of agreements which allow key suppliers direct access to Wal-Mart data. As a result, the benefits of "just in time" inventory management can now be applied to retailing situations, not just manufacturing.

The process improvements in inventory management have come from an understanding of the value of data and its use. This is true for processes that have a significant manual component, such as the initial Japanese *Kanban* methods. It is also true for processes like those used by Wal-Mart and the Port of Singapore, where automation has provided improvements through increased accuracy, reduced process costs, and created greater customer satisfaction.

Value Through Better Financial Management

One of the most obvious areas where data processing provides value to the enterprise is in the management of financial and accounting information. This differs, to some extent, from the value generated by savings in manpower and inventory, because it provides the enterprise with opportunities to actually increase revenues as well as assistance in avoiding unnecessary costs.

In establishing asset value for the equipment management system and its data, the financial benefits were indirect. The system enabled the telephone company to install service more quickly than had been done previously. A wait of several days for telephone service had been reduced in some cases to a matter of hours. This meant that the telephone equipment was being used in a revenue-generating manner for a higher percentage of the time.

In the end, we decided against assigning a value for the increased revenue attributable to the system because we felt that the majority of the value had been generated by improved field engineering practices. Although the computerization of the equipment data had played a significant role in supporting the changes in engineering practices, the heart of the change was the business decision to handle all routine connections and disconnections through the central office, rather than out in the field. The business decision was, in many ways, the outcome of regulatory changes that resulted in telephone users owning their own telephones. The telephone company no longer needed to send a serviceman to the user location to install or retrieve telephone company equipment. Since all of these factors were involved, we felt that it would be impossible to substantiate a claim that the system was responsible for a given percentage of the benefits from the changed practices.

The reduction in unused inventory also had an indirect financial impact, since it meant that the amount of financing could be reduced. This, in turn, lowered interest payments and increased earnings accordingly. Again, we decided against an attempt to quantify these benefits because we believed that some of the carrying costs were already embedded in the inventory valuation.

For systems that are primarily concerned with handling financial and accounting data, the increased value of the system can be established in many ways. Some examples are:

- Improved cash management that allows idle corporate funds to be invested and earn interest income.

- Improved management of both accounts payable and receivable, that can reduce the amount of float in the company's financial position. For a very large company the cost of money associated with this float can run into millions of dollars.

- Improved credit management, that can reduce the level of write-offs.

- •Comprehensive reporting, allowing problems in business unit performance to be identified before they get out of hand.
- •Reduced costs in preparation of the reports that are required by governmental or other agencies.
- •Improved budget tracking for activities within the enterprise.
- •Improved information that can be used in preparing sales and production plans.
- •And, of course, the reduction in staff needed to manage the financial information.

The specific approach taken to establish the value for financial data that has been captured in automated form should correspond to the way in which the financial data is currently reported for operational use. Financial departments within organizations can be expected to have a great deal of insight into the value of the data in their work and to the organization as a whole. In my experience I have found the financial groups to be very supportive in attempts to determine an asset value for the data they use. There seems to be a clear understanding that the worth of the financial organization to the enterprise can only be strengthened by pointing out the value of the data they use in their business process.

We have become so accustomed to the presence of financial systems in our daily work that their effect is often overlooked. Because financial operations in an enterprise are so pervasive, it may be difficult to develop an asset value that includes all of the benefits brought about by computerization. A more serious problem may be that the benefits are so great that their value simply will not be believed once it has been determined.

Information as a Product

In some cases the improved management of data (made possible through the use of computer systems) has enabled companies to offer services and products to customers that would otherwise not be available. Telephone companies have developed sophisticated billing and reporting options that provide real value to their customers, such as consolidated billing for customers with telephones in several locations, calling plans that give discounts based on patterns of use, and special event rates, such as a discount for long-distance calls on Mother's Day. These are all services that could not have been administered without computerized management of telephone data.

Telecommunications customers regard the information that the telephone companies can provide as an important element in their attempts to control operating costs. The variety of information that the telephone company provides has become a crucial factor in closing sales.

In some cases the benefits of data processing are even more dramatic. Competitive Media Reporting, Inc., (formerly Broadcast Advertisers Reports) tracks commercials on radio and television. It does this in seventy-five cities and can report to each advertiser how many times their commercials ran, whether the commercials were broadcast completely, which commercials ran before them and after them. Advertisers can also learn how many of the competitor's commercials ran, where they were run, whether or not this represents a change in the competitor's advertising pattern, and a number of other facts that are of interest to companies that advertise heavily.

Competitive Media Reporting became the dominant firm in their field by constantly examining the data that they were collecting. As they studied it they postulated ways in which it could be used by their customers. They took these ideas to their customers and developed new products. Their business continued to grow. When a national media survey company announced plans to challenge Competitive Media Reporting, the response was, "Let 'em try." The survey company tried. They didn't succeed.

Putting a Value on "Soft" Contributions

How does one establish a value for the data processing contribution in these cases? In the case of Competitive Media Reporting, where the data is the primary product of the company, the exercise may not be necessary. The value of the data can be measured directly by looking at the company's revenue stream. Without the data, there would be no revenue.

In the case of the revenue contribution made by telephone company billing and reporting flexibility, any attempt to develop a hard number is probably doomed to failure. In practice it has been acceptable to assign a small percentage of increased sales to the data processing operation. In our evaluation of the equipment management system, we set the contribution value at two percent. We wanted to establish the fact that data processing was a contributor to additional sales on a consistent basis. We hoped that this would give us a future opportunity to examine ways in which the contribution could be increased.

Quantifying impact on savings or revenue for a particular function such as data processing can be difficult. In many enterprises such contributions are treated as non-financial benefits. There may be little support for efforts to assign monetary value to Data Processing contributions.

If you believe that Data Processing has made a contribution to revenue or has played a role in reducing cost, then you must find a way to quantify it. Make the contribution or reduction as conservative as you want to and be prepared to give some examples. Examples that were used to support the claim of a two percent contribution to sales based on improved telephone bills included:

- The fact that billing flexibility and options were featured in advertising materials.

- The number of calls from sales to the billing systems group asking about features or modifications for specific customers.

- The number of requests for additional features that were initiated by the sales group.

- The fact that articles on the importance of billing options and flexibility had appeared with regularity in telecommunications trade journals.

- The number of training sessions and presentations requested by marketing, including those which included potential customers.

By using information like this it was possible to establish a strong case that billing systems were making a contribution to additional sales. The case was presented to the sales group and they agreed. They also agreed that we should consider ways to make the contribution greater in the future.

Treating the Systems as Sources of Value

How do we put a value on the software that provides organization and access to the data we have been discussing? Surely it has an intrinsic value. The manner in which our software works often has a direct bearing on the work processes. A bad implementation can make the data less valuable because the system does not provide the proper access to it. A good implementation can mean that users embrace the system and find new and better ways of using it, further increasing the value of the data.

I take the position that the software is similar to the hardware in that it happens to be the environment where the data lives today. I believe that the software has value only to the extent that it directly produces revenue through its sale or lease. All other value is reflected in the actual improvements to the business processes. For that purpose the value of the software is indistinguishable from the value of the data that it manages.

Since software has cost, as does computer hardware, that cost must be considered in determining a net asset value for the data and systems used in the enterprise. Amazingly, we were never able to determine software cost to the same degree of accuracy as we did for system and data value. I believe this is a function of the age of the system. A great deal of functionality is added to systems over time, and much of that functionality results from the software maintenance process. The allocation of funds to systems in the software maintenance process is very imprecise in the majority of enterprises that I have studied. My discussions with software maintainers in other companies leads me to believe that this situation is widespread.

One significant situation in which the software and hardware have an intrinsic value beyond their cost is in the area of embedded systems. In these systems hardware and software are incorporated as parts of a larger product that is then sold as a unit. The perceived value of the product to its customers will be directly influenced by the software and hardware, and not by a store of data. The price of the system will reflect this value.

The degree to which this value can be treated as an asset is another issue. Embedded software and hardware are like inventory items to be consumed. It is only when such software is constructed so it can be reused (and thus contribute to many products over an extended period) that it can be regarded as the same type of asset as the corporate marketing and sales data. It is important to note that software technology is changing to support a higher level of reuse than has been typical in the past. Techniques such as object-oriented software construction and the use of code generators that allow software to be maintained at the level of reusable design will allow today's software to yield a recurring value by providing cost avoidance in future systems. As this happens the software can and should be treated as an asset.

A proprietary technique or algorithm that is embodied in the software is another issue. Although these situations are unusual, in those cases where they do occur the system that implements the algorithm or technique should be valued as an asset, and it should be clearly recognized as a source of recurring benefits.

It is interesting to note that some of America's major telecommunications companies have changed their opinions as to whether systems or data constitute the asset to be managed. Five years ago, "systems assets" groups were brought into being by Data Processing departments in AT&T and some of the larger independent companies. These groups were chartered to identify computer software systems that exhibited both high quality and sufficient flexibility to allow them to be used over an extended period of time.

Funds were made available to create improved documentation and create software asset libraries that could be accessed by future software developers.

Today, one of AT&T's major divisions identifies the data it manages as its most significant asset. This has led, in turn, to a new emphasis on the data as a source of business opportunities—something that is difficult to do with software systems.

An Unresolved Issue

There are situations where data contributes directly to savings and revenue enhancement, but where it is difficult to think of the data as an asset. An example would be a data feed from a commodities exchange that was then scanned by a system which, in turn, dynamically computed trends or transmitted notices when specified transactions or price levels were detected.

The company that uses the feed does not create the data it contains. One could argue that the computed trend values consist of data that supplies a recurring benefit to the company, but I think that this sort of reasoning stretches credibility.

How do we go about assigning a value to this data? It doesn't make sense to think of the incoming data feed as an asset that can be managed by the companies who use it. Nevertheless, it is critically important to the company that the data stream be available. It might be useful to know how much benefit is being generated and then make a comparison to the cost of the data service. However, it is not clear that this information would yield any insights that could be applied to management decisions affecting future systems planning.

As enterprises make more and more use of data resources that they do not own or control, it may become more worthwhile to determine the value of each of the resources. This value can then be used as a control mechanism to ensure that data access services are not being renewed after they have lost their value.

Making the Measurement an Open Process

You need to remember that determining the asset value of the company's information is something that probably hasn't been done before. Many people will wonder what you are doing and many of them will initially suspect your motives.

I have found that the straightforward approach in dealing with the people who must help you in establishing asset value is particularly useful. First, it can be understood by virtually anyone you talk to and, second, it provides a good opening for more extended discussion about the role of Data Processing vis-a-vis other parts of the enterprise.

The straightforward approach goes as follows:

- There's a lot of data on the computers

- The company spends a great deal of money collecting this data

- The data is used by people when they do their jobs

- Therefore, the data must be worth something

- We don't know how much it's worth

- How much it's worth depends on how it's used

- We want to know how data is used in different parts of the company

- We want to find out what changes have occurred over time since the data was made more readily available by using computers

- We want to use what we learn to focus data processing resources in the areas where data processing is most important

- We want to cut data processing costs by getting rid of activities that don't provide enough benefit

The straightforward approach can be understood by everyone, from the janitor to the CEO. The things you will be doing as you gather data can be related directly back to what you said you were going to do. The admission that you don't know what the data's worth will be believed by everybody. They don't know what it's worth, either.

The process of finding out how data is used and tracing the impact it has had on the organizations which use it can give the Data Processing group an excellent insight into the way that its products are actually used. Far too often such information is available today only through second-hand anecdotes and problem reports.

This raises the issue of recording the research so that it can be reused. Determining asset value is simply too much work to be redone from scratch to support an annual budget process. I discuss enterprise models in a later chapter, but for now the important thing to realize is that the output from the valuation effort is a model. The model tells you what has happened to a business process through better use of data and traces both the nature and volume of the impact.

It is the initial creation of the model that takes so much time and effort. Maintaining it is much easier. As a Data Processing manager you should be in a position to identify the data you need to update the model. You will know where to get the data and you will know how to apply it. The people you are sharing the outputs with will understand the approach and will be able to focus on the implications of the most recent changes.

The work of keeping the asset models vigorous should be a task handled directly by the person at the highest executive level within the Data Processing organization. At this level of the organization the asset approach to funding will have its greatest impact. The knowledge embedded in the models will be of great value in helping the Data Processing executive communicate effectively with her peers in manufacturing, finance, personnel or other divisions of the enterprise.

Like any other process improvement, you have to apply data at the point in the process where it will have the greatest effect.

A Question of Accuracy

Since much of the work which establishes the savings or revenue contribution of systems and data depends upon the determination of a degree of contribution, the accuracy of the final value can always be challenged. When we say that the availability of data in the computer has contributed eighty-five percent of the overall improvement in the service ordering process, we have applied a semi-relative judgement to yield what looks like an absolute number.

The judgement is semi-relative because, if we have done the work correctly, we will be able to state the percentage of our orders that originate from existing customers and for those orders, the degree to which data entry time is cut for the customer information portion. We will have hard evidence that on-line prompting for item numbers has reduced the line item entry time from over three minutes per item to under fifteen seconds. All this is quantifiable and can be strongly defended.

The gains become harder to quantify if company is receiving increased orders from purchasing agents who already know in detail which items they want and what discounts apply. This means less work for the order entry personnel and looks like productivity improvement, but it can't be linked directly to the improvements in the order process brought about by automation.

As a result, when we get down to the hard business of choosing a value for the contribution, we have to make some judgement calls. By basing most of the contribution on factors that can be directly measured, the accuracy of the values becomes easier to prove. If the contribution attributed to soft factors is below ten percent, there should be no problem with challenges to the overall accuracy of the analysis.

In many cases a challenge to the accuracy of the asset valuation process comes from those who feel that the support they receive from the Data Processing group is in danger of being cut back. I don't know of any consistently reliable way to deal with political attacks directed against quantitative analysis. The only action that seems to have any success in blunting these challenges is an offer to re-visit the analysis as it applies to the business processes of interest to the people or organizations who challenge the asset valuation.

Converting Process Improvement to Asset Value

The key is to identify the recurring benefits. In the case of Central Office Assignment, the improvements in productivity meant that fewer people were needed. This was a recurring benefit. Consistently lower levels of inventory are another form of recurring benefit. The additional income gained from better cash management, as supported by the company's financial systems, is a recurring benefit whose value may vary based on external factors, such as interest rates—but it is a recurring benefit.

Think of the recurring benefits from process improvement as a form of interest payment. Let's say the telephone company's equipment management system yielded six million dollars in benefits each year. Subtract the one million dollars it cost to run and maintain the equipment management system during the year. There is now a five million dollar net annual benefit for having the equipment data and the systems that administer it.

If current long-term interest rates are eight percent, the size of the deposit necessary to yield the five million dollar net benefit is sixty-two and a half million dollars. The company is realizing five dollars net benefit for every dollar invested (one million dollars cost, five million dollars net benefit). This is an excellent rate of return in anybody's book. Furthermore, the company is investing only 1.6 percent of the asset value on an annual basis in order to obtain this return.

The long-term funding approach that we pursued was to establish a reinvestment level for the system and data as a fixed percentage of its asset value. A two percent reinvestment would yield a budget of one and a quarter million dollars for operation, maintenance, and enhancement. As the performance of the Data Processing team improved and the enhancements increased the value of the asset, the amount reinvested in the systems and data would continue to increase.

Take the Money and Run?

Showing the worth of the data and using that worth as the basis for a substantial and stable budget request may unlock funding which can be applied to the unglamorous but ultimately essential tasks that maintain systems integrity, improve systems and data quality, and improve the long-term value of the information asset. It makes sense to state these plans explicitly along with the budget request and justification.

Projects such as reverse engineering for critical systems, conversion of databases from several different database management systems to a common one, data usage evaluation, and a score of others often languish because it is not possible to show a direct payoff in a finite time-frame. The use of asset-based funding allows a portion of the budget to be assigned to these reinvestment activities without requiring an explicit quantification of benefits.

The work required to develop the asset value will help you identify areas that can benefit most from additional attention.   In many cases you will find ways in which the value of the data could be improved by combining or streamlining functions. The data users who assisted you in the analysis will often be the ones who will alert you to these possibilities for improvement.

The areas that benefit from improvement may not be the problem areas that are related to a stream of enhancement requests. They may well be in areas where users and technical staff feel that earlier problems have been solved and have neglected to expand their horizons to see what might be possible with a bit more work.

Do not assume that every attempt to prove the asset value of a set of data will yield an impressive amount. In some cases, you may complete your analysis only to realize that a system is actually costing more than it is worth. If this happens, don't look on it as a setback. By recommending that the system in question be downsized or eliminated, you should be able to overcome executive doubts as to whether the asset approach is simply another ploy to increase Data Processing budgets.

The Asset Advantage

The information asset approach we used in the telephone equipment management systems analysis had two significant advantages over the project oriented approach that it supplanted. First, it circumvented the usual difficulties in obtaining funding for long-term, non-glamorous activities such as incremental system improvement and broad-based initiatives to improve systems quality. We established that there was a high payoff for investing in the equipment management data and system. Since that the benefit was historically proven rather than projected, funding could be provided on a strategic basis rather than on a project basis. This pulled the funding out of the cost/benefit auction.

Second, the linkage between asset value and funding served as an incentive for the people who managed the system and data to look for ways in which the asset value could be increased. This was different than previous practice, where the systems managers simply reacted as best they could to user requests.

The importance of both of these benefits is difficult to overstate. Systems and data with long-term strategic importance can benefit greatly from stable long-term funding. This type of funding makes it possible to undertake broad-based quality improvement initiatives as well as essential but low-visibility activities that fare poorly in the cost/benefit auctions that usually determine project funding.

When the strategic importance of such systems is recognized and quantified, it focuses the attention of both Data Processing and other areas of company management on the systems and data that are doing the most for the enterprise. These systems are often held in low esteem when flashy new projects are on the horizon. Who wants to work on improvements to the inventory system when a state-of-the-art, workstation-based Executive Information System is in the offing?

Knowing what today's data and systems are actually contributing to the enterprise helps everyone who works with them make better decisions today about data and systems investment for tomorrow.

4

Cost/Benefit Analysis and Other Myths

Suppose you have just been selected to do a cost/benefit analysis for developing some new computer software. For the foreseeable future, you will be bombarded with questions about how you developed your numbers, whether you considered various obscure factors, the degree to which you examined all possible (and even impossible) alternatives, and whether you are willing to provide an iron-clad guarantee of accuracy. You will be asked to rearrange your numbers, graphs and presentations and will spend many hours in meetings. You will wonder if anyone understands what they are putting you through and you will come to believe that nobody does, and even if they did, they wouldn't care.

Cost/benefit studies, also called justifications, analyses, and exercises, have been the bane of Data Processing managers for years. The odd thing is that very few managers have realized that the deck is stacked against them from the beginning. The current cost/benefit mechanism has fundamental structural flaws and until they are corrected, it will continue to play a major role in derailing the effective management of the information asset.

Let's start at the beginning. Systems themselves do not provide benefits. All that a system can do is support the practices that constitute a business process. It is the practices the system supports that provide the benefits to the enterprise.

There is a benefit to reducing the amount of work necessary to trace an order. An order tracking system can contribute to the reduction in work, but the system itself does not provide the benefit. Using the system, a clerk can look up order information while on the phone with a customer instead of having to find the files and call back. The system ensures that files are not misplaced or unavailable. With the system supporting the order tracking process, less physical space and fewer people are required. Because the system makes data available to the clerks in a fast and accurate manner, the order tracking process can be redesigned to lower cost and provide better customer service.

As a Data Processing manager you are responsible for the system, not the order tracking process. Why would you try to place a value on the benefits of improved order tracking? The answer is simple—you shouldn't! The benefits, both quantitative and qualitative, should be supplied by the managers who will use the system.

Let's face facts. In most companies, Data Processing is a cost center rather than a profit center. Even in those cases where your users ostensibly "buy" Data Processing services from you, all that really happens is that the costs of Data Processing are allocated throughout the rest of the organization. Either way, your operation represents a drain on the profit centers. No wonder they want you to provide more service for the money they're paying for Data Processing support.

The first step toward rational systems planning is to understand where requests for development or enhancement are coming from, and to discover what the incentive for them really is. If you are the one who is required to project the benefits for system development or improvement, you may find you are advocating a system that the user doesn't really want or understand. Examine the work being considered and spend some time to learn where the initiative to do it originated. Is this a project which is really sponsored by the user? If so, which user?

Whose Benefits Are These, Anyway?

Once you identify the sponsor (or sponsors) for a systems project, you should demand that she (they) work with you to project the benefits. This action alone will kill a lot of half-baked ideas. Be particularly cautious about projects for which you are the sponsor, or ones for which somebody in the Data Processing group recruited a sponsor. Many technically interesting projects get started simply because of a fascination with what is possible.

Since benefits are always estimated, you need to spend time with the user (or sponsor) to understand what goes into the estimates. Find out what's behind the statement that, "…this enhancement will save us $13.7 million over the next three years." Very seldom will there be only one source of benefit. Remember the 80-20 rule: 80 percent of the benefit will be obtained from 20 percent of the functionality. Work with the user to identify the 20 percent of the functionality that is most critical.

You should be particularly cautious if the sponsor can't identify the functionality that will provide the bulk of the benefit. Data Processing people are not the only ones who become dazzled by technical possibilities. Try to work with the sponsor so that you completely understand the role of the system in obtaining the benefit. This will help you to better understand what must be done on the system in order to give the sponsor what she really needs.

And at the end of all this activity, no matter how conscientious you have been in your work, you will probably wind up with a report which is all but useless.

It's Not the Analyses That are Bad, It's the Process

In many companies cost/benefit studies are used as pawns in a game to determine who gets funding and who doesn't. "Substantial benefits, low risk, quick pay-back" has become a joke at many companies. No project is going to claim anything else. The cost/benefit analysis used to support requests for funding will be adjusted to support the pre-determined conclusion — that a new system is needed. This is merely a way of dressing up company politics with spreadsheet printouts. If you agree to play this sort of game you are signing up to play politics for life — or at least for the remainder of your career with your current employer. If that's what you want, fine. Just don't kid yourself.

Things can be even worse if the cost/benefit process is used as a parade ground for political prowess. Destructive though it may be, estimates of costs and benefits are often used as poker chips in an effort to convince corporate executives that one individual or the other is more committed or a better risk taker. In an organization that makes a habit of reassigning managers every couple of years, such posturing becomes a can't lose exercise for the person making the projections. By the time things fall apart she will no longer be in charge of the effort.

Assuming that political machinations are at a non-destructive level, you should try to look objectively at the larger process of funding systems activity as well as the role of cost/benefit analysis in that process. You will realize quickly that cost/benefit analyses are not done unless there's competition for funds. If adequate money is available and the project under consideration is relatively limited in scope, it's not uncommon to get started on the basis of a memorandum.

Take the time to think about what the cost/benefit process is really doing. Is it supporting an overall plan to improve the performance of the enterprise? Is it providing an objective evaluation of alternative systems strategies? Is it *really* contributing to a rational planning process? In many companies the answer is no. Cost/benefit analyses are used to justify systems development or modification to support a specific business process. They are advocacy documents, pure and simple. Many of the systems that cause you problems today began their lives as the subject of a cost/benefit analysis.

As you analyze the cost/benefit process, you will see that costs and benefits are usually drawn up within a closed project boundary. There may be some discussion of non-financial benefits or intangibles which lie outside the boundaries of the project, but the focus of the study will be clearly drawn. Reports and presentations associated with the analysis will emphasize these boundaries in an attempt to clarify the project. This is fine and good as far as it goes, but for the people who must do the funding allocation, it's like receiving an unassembled jigsaw puzzle.

It is no more possible to successfully implement a rational systems funding policy by evaluating individual systems than to design a successful sports car by carefully examining the components. In the majority of enterprises, the major flaw of the cost/benefit approach to systems funding is that it operates in a vacuum.

Several "leading edge" companies are making attempts to broaden the base of systems planning. I know of one major corporation which has spent a great deal of time and money developing interlocking methodologies to govern systems development and Data Processing project management. The methodologies involve the definition of strategic programs that support programs and systems. Unfortunately, the clean and precise structure of the methodologies breaks down in practice. Proposed systems are found to be linked to multiple supporting programs which in turn support multiple strategic programs. The claims of benefits stagnate as very high-level generalities because the process is administered by System Planners, Common Architecture Planners and System Developers. Users are represented only indirectly. The words in the methodologies sound as if there is broad participation by all parties. The reality is that the methodologies have been taken over by the technicians. The cost/benefit analyses that emerge from the process are no more relevant than they were before the methodologies and their attendants were put in place.

The Potential for Change

Cost/Benefit Analysis sounds so reasonable and rational that it's difficult to convince anyone that the process, as it is generally implemented, is self-defeating. The usual approach is to attempt to fine tune the methodology to deal with observable inconsistencies. When all the analysis work is followed by irrational funding decisions, shoulders are shrugged and the technicians mutter under their breath about the "idiots up on mahogany row." The idea that this idiocy is a natural by-product of relying on project-based cost/benefit studies never seems to be recognized.

A cost/benefit analysis process that identifies *all* of the costs and benefits for each project within a common framework *will* support a rational systems planning and funding policy. However, this kind of process must be much more than an amalgam of existing individual cost/benefit studies. The thousand-piece jigsaw puzzle doesn't suddenly become easier if you add another thousand pieces.

In the first place, the cost/benefit process needs to become a *discovery* tool rather than an *advocacy* tool. It needs to be used to validate assumptions about the benefits and costs of a project. Specific cause-and-effect benefits must be identified and side-effects must be clearly described. One tool for supporting the discovery process is an enterprise model or business process model. Admittedly, development of these models is neither easy nor cheap, but the cost of continuing the current funding practices is almost certain to be more expensive over time.

The presence of an effective model—one which can be understood by users as well as Data Processing people—also shows the way in which multiple projects affect each other. This facet of analysis is completely absent from the current project-based approach. It's a facet which needs to be considered if there is to be any realistic attempt to develop and implement a long-term technical strategy.

Improving the Cost/Benefit Process As It Is Today

Although there are tools and techniques that can be used to change the nature of cost/benefit analysis (so that it can start to actually perform the task for which it was intended) it's unlikely that they will be available tomorrow morning. This means that you, as a representative of Data Processing, will still be involved in creating narrowly focused cost/benefit studies. You will also have to live with the consequences. As President Carter said, "Life is unfair."

This is not the time to quit. It's time to initiate actions that will improve the funding environment.

First, get your part of the cost/benefit process in order. You shouldn't let the problems with the overall systems funding process deter you from improving your ability to estimate the costs of designing, implementing and maintaining software. Since the mid-1980's there has been an increasing amount of research and information dealing with ways to improve the technical aspects of the software processes where you do exercise some direct influence.

Techniques for improving the quality of design and implementation are becoming more widely practiced. Their sophistication is increasing. Code generators, integrated CASE, and rich development environments (particularly for graphic user interfaces) can substantially improve productivity and product quality when they are used in a disciplined manner.

The software process itself has been modeled and analyzed. Data is available on systems complexity, software quality and programmer productivity. There are many books and articles dealing with software development methodologies.

Progress in the art of estimation has lagged behind these developments. Most Data Processing organizations have not yet introduced consistent measurement metrics on which to base estimates. Most Data Processing project managers have no exposure to established tools that can help with the estimation task. Because of this, there is a natural inclination to discount the value of cost estimates produced by the Data Processing staff. Unfortunately, there is often nothing else available to corporate management or DP steering committees when it comes time to select those projects to be undertaken from the set of projects that were proposed. The lack of confidence in the estimates sometimes leads to the irrational decisions which drive Data Processing managers to distraction.

The Data Processing staff has a responsibility to ensure that apples are being compared to apples on the cost side. Consistent estimating practices are of key importance and development of checklists can make the job easier as well. If your users understand how you develop cost estimates, their fear that you are "tweaking" the costs to ensure approval of work which you are interested in will be reduced.

It is worth the time and effort involved to adopt a standard estimating method and use it consistently. Methods such as the Constructive Cost Model (CoCoMo) and "Bang" are well documented and can be explained to those who question the manner in which the estimates were derived. Even better is the Function Point Analysis method because it relates more directly to the user's perception of what the parts of the system are. Unless your company has been collecting data about system development activities for an extended period of time, you should adopt an industry standard estimating method which is recognized as providing a reasonable level of accuracy. The problem with almost all home-grown methodologies is that the urge to keep changing them is hard to resist.

Once you have decided upon a method, make sure that you allocate time to explain it to everyone who relies on your estimates. You are a technical executive developing estimates for work that many other managers don't understand. Your cost and benefit presentations will be subjected to considerable scrutiny. Make sure you have answers for the inevitable questions.

Don't be afraid to take the offensive. The fact that you have implemented a standard estimating process and are using that process to improve the quality of your work should be used as a prod to change other aspects of the funding process. A demonstrated ability to improve the effectiveness of the Data Processing activity, as evidenced by the fact that you improve your ability to deliver systems within original budget and time estimates, is the strongest possible support for your credibility. This is important when you try to influence others to exchange the current cost/benefit process with an asset-based approach.

As you work to implement improvements to the software process, make sure that members of your own staff become believers as well. They will create part of the source material for the estimates and their understanding of the process will help them to provide more accurate and appropriate data about the work that needs to be done. Knowing the way in which estimates are being developed reassures the technical staff that they will not be handed an unrealistic schedule as a result of some off-the-cuff opinion that a requested change shouldn't be too difficult.

Make sure that your assumptions are clearly documented and are presented as part of the cost estimates. Document sources and quality of data, access to business process expertise, availability of human and electronic resources, and key technical aspects of the project. Projects have a way of changing which invalidates initial assumptions, and it's important to have some leverage that can be applied to those who would change everything in the project except the budget and completion date.

There is a real value for both the Data Processing group and the enterprise as a whole in improving the software process. First, you will be directly contributing to the growth of the enterprise's information asset. Second, the improvements will be needed as you improve the Data Processing funding process over time. No matter how the benefits are calculated, it will still be necessary to estimate the Data Processing costs.

As an individual issue it's important to move your enterprise to the position where they regard Data Processing as an asset management function rather than a cost center. Managers who control the assets of the enterprise have the highest visibility and the inside track on career advancement. As long as data processing is viewed as being strictly a support organization, the leadership potential of those who manage it will be discounted.

Many Data Processing managers have adopted the mantle of "supporters to more important parts of the business." This is self-constraining. Examples of successful corporate executives who have used Data Processing as a base for their advancement can be found in leading edge firms in banking, transportation, publishing and retailing. The fact is that these firms have taken advantage of improved information use to become pacesetters in their industries. The pressure to obtain competitive advantage from Data Processing is likely to come to your enterprise as well. If you regard Data Processing as strictly a support function, you won't be seriously considered as a candidate for a leadership position.

For the near term, the best way (the only way?) to survive the cost/benefit gauntlet is to make sure that the cost/benefit study is a joint effort between you and your users. The best thing you can do for your staff and the enterprise that employs you is to recognize the things that the current cost/benefit mechanism cannot do and to work toward implementing a new process which improves the information asset instead of dissecting it.

5

Less
Than
Expected

Delivered systems often fail to meet expectations. This is not always the fault of the systems. Sometimes expectations are so great that no buildable system could meet them. This is scant consolation to people who have labored to create a good system only to be met with user disappointment and complaints.

Technical managers within the Data Processing organization need to understand the nature of user expectations and of their own role in shaping and controlling these expectations. The problem of unrealistic expectations cannot be expected to cure itself.

The problem starts, as most serious problems do, at the beginning of the process. When a system is to be built or enhanced, one of the first problems to be solved is that of obtaining the funding to do the work. This normally involves development of some sort of cost and benefit analysis.

Almost without exception, the cost and benefit analysis is an advocacy document dressed up to look like an objective study. In most cases, both costs and benefits are projected from a combination of current data and underlying assumptions. These assumptions are used to emphasize certain aspects of the project and to minimize others. Although the work of putting the best face on the project falls to people in staff positions, what comes out of the process is carried forward by their managers.

The seed of the problem is this—during the cost and benefit analysis questions regarding the underlying assumptions are discussed openly, and the people participating in the analysis develop an understanding of the risks that are being injected into the analytical process. Problems related to organizational conflicts, the level of readiness to adopt a new technology, current levels of productivity and the quality of management are likely to be debated at some length. Past failures are dredged up in an attempt to see whether the enterprise learned from them or is doomed to repeat them. The analysis of the potential of a new system to help the enterprise is often a manic proceeding, oscillating between deep pessimism and wild enthusiasm—often within a matter of hours. Participants attempt to judge the potential of the project as it relates to their own career goals or the aspirations of the groups of which they are members. It becomes increasingly difficult to stay objective.

As the time allotted for analysis draws to a close, pressure builds to present an optimistic picture of the systems project. It seems that there is always a way to do this when the boss requests it. The doubts and concerns are excised or watered down to make the analysis results non-controversial and the "objective" report is issued. It is through this report and the way it is presented that the project becomes known to management and users. It is this adulterated view that will be used to compare the project to other projects (also known through adulterated views) in the process that determines which of them will get the money to go forward.

Writing in *Software Magazine*, Francis Pascarella of Chain Bridge Systems captures what really goes on. "Unfortunately, too many companies have found more reasons to rationalize systems automation than to cost-justify it. Instead of setting tangible milestones, they manipulate data to provide tantalizing reports." Managers who have responsibility for directing a business process are usually under pressure from their superiors to improve the effectiveness of the process. An attempt to increase the Data Processing content of the process is often viewed as a proactive step. If the hoped-for improvement doesn't materialize, the manager who initiated the computer project stands a good chance of successfully shifting the blame for the shortcomings onto the Data Processing group.

For systems work requested by a department that is ready and willing to fund the work, the analysis team may be reluctant to state that there may be difficulties in providing all of the requested functionality and all of the projected benefit. In these situations, the user may pressure the team to issue a superficial report that focuses exclusively on the positive aspects of the project. Later, if the projected benefits don't materialize, the analysis team can find itself castigated for inadequate work.

There is rarely a conscious attempt to deceive by the staff which does the cost and benefit work. If the issue of downplaying the negative aspects of the project comes up, it is usually rationalized by showcasing the preponderance of possible benefits. The general feeling is usually that any required course corrections can be made after funding is locked in.

The Data Processing staff often plays a key role in inflating expectations at this point. By pointing out the many linkages that can be established between the new systems or enhancements and the systems that are already in place, an assumption of "synergistic benefit" can be made. If the new project offers the chance of using new technology or methods, the effectiveness of these methods will be assumed from whatever published material is available—generally advertising. Doing new things is fun, and it takes a hard-hearted attitude to turn down the chance to have some fun.

It's not only Data Processing staff who will become interested in new technologies. As news and publicity surrounding hardware and software tools becomes more noticeable in business publications, managers who are requesting systems work will often include suggestions about the tools that should be used to carry it out.

The benefits ascribed to the project take on a life of their own when they leave the staff who identified them. An executive who receives a system proposal containing claims of significant improvements in productivity or substantial cost reductions will focus on the benefits—both to the enterprise and to her career. If the project contains a "silver bullet" in the form of technological advances, it becomes that much more believable.

Enthusiasm at the executive level can be contagious. The people who worked on the original cost and benefit analysis may feel that the claimed benefits are being inflated, but it is a safe bet that none of them will step forward to point out the risks which were earlier minimized. There are few warm feelings for the weatherman who announces that it will rain on the day of the parade.

This is a very difficult situation for the Data Processing group and its managers. If they make statements that try to tone down expectations, such statements may be taken as attempts to get out from under prior commitments. Particularly in larger companies, there is a lot of pressure on managers to be team players if they want to advance their careers.

Where's the Lifeboat?

Bad projects are like briar patches. It is much easier to not get into them in the first place than it is to extricate yourself once you are stuck in the middle. And, like briar patches, they yield a continuous sequence of bothersome cuts and rips. With projects, these cuts and rips are not on skin and fabric, but on the enthusiasm, patience, creativity and dedication of the technical and management staff. Data Processing management needs ways to quickly back out if the first step on the project leads into a nest of thorns.

It is at the point where the proposal is starting to take on a life of its own that a clear and concise requirements document is worth its weight in gold. If the requirements document is riddled with generalities or is difficult to understand, Data Processing management should immediately act to develop a readable abstract and presentation from the available material. Few requirements documents contain explicit statements about what the system will *not* do. Make sure the abstract has this information.

A readable abstract is one that can be read and understood by people in the user and executive community. There needs to be a conscious effort to keep techno-speak out. There also needs to be a conscious effort to keep the abstract and requirements document neutral. Restrain yourself if you are tempted to overreact in an attempt to slow down a project you feel is ill-advised. I do not know of one instance where a Data Processing manager was able to kill a poorly conceived systems initiative by making it a personal issue, but I have seen this approach seriously wound some promising careers.

Armed with the abstract and presentation, the Data Processing manager must take a proactive position with users and executive management. She must *insist* that they be present for one or more milestone presentations, if necessary by threatening to stop work on the project until a properly attended milestone presentation has taken place. At each of these presentations she must correlate what has been done so far with the functionality that is eventually going to be delivered. She must deliver a clear message about what the system will do and what it won't do.

This is the time to openly discuss risks associated with the project. In this forum the risks act as a counterpoint to the progress that has been announced. As such, identification of the risks will appear as the prudent and conservative act that it is.

Another excellent way of managing user expectations is to ensure that users are properly represented in the system testing and acceptance process. The users who participate may be disappointed that the system they are testing falls short of their initial expectations, but they are unlikely to be unpleasantly surprised at what the system does when it is finally put into production. If users are badly disappointed early in the process, they may take the initiative to call for a reevaluation of the project. More often, their reactions will extend the project so that changes can be made in order to make the system more suitable for eventual use.

A combination of disappointment and surprise from the user community at the unveiling of a new system is the kiss of death for Data Processing managers. Surprise is fine if there is no disappointment. Disappointment can be managed if there is no surprise. However, when both occur together the only conclusion that the users and executives of the company will reach is that someone in Data Processing has not been forthright and honest. This conclusion damages everyone associated with it.

The only way to manage expectations so that they don't get out of control is to doggedly insist on communicating with users and executives. If the project is on schedule and is meeting the requirements approved for it, there can be a great temptation to believe that the job of selling the system to management and users has been completed. Nothing could be further from the truth.

Stopping the selling process when the technical work starts is the same as setting cruise control on your car and then settling back for a nap. There's likely to be a rude awakening.

6

The Philosopher's Stone

In the middle ages alchemists looked for the Philosopher's Stone. They believed it had the power to transmute base metals into gold. The same search goes on today in Data Processing groups. The only difference is that the Philosopher's Stone is now called "Executive Commitment."

I have lost track of the times I have heard Executive Commitment invoked for its all-healing power:

> *"Without executive commitment, the benefits of this new methodology can never be fully realized."*

> *"We need to have solid support at the highest executive levels for this program to succeed."*

> *"We thought that upper management was committed when we started this turkey. I guess we were wrong."*

What is this executive commitment? It appears that it means very different things to Data Processing management and to the actual corporate executives. This is often reflected in the way that DP managers look for signs of favor. Was a presentation asked for? Was there a suggestion to run the idea past another Vice-President? The Data Processing group studies these signs the same way that Western intelligence services studied the line of men standing over Lenin's tomb on May Day. In both cases, there is a lack of understanding about what's going on.

So, what *is* going on?

Corporate executives don't have a commitment to the Data Processing staff any more than they have one to the building maintenance staff. Their commitment is to the business as a whole: to the owners, customers, and employees of the enterprise. During the course of business operations, they will focus their attention on some aspects of the enterprise while leaving other aspects alone.

When they seek executive commitment what the DP group is usually asking for is a blank check: a statement that the corporation will see the project through, no matter what happens. The executives are not being asked to approve DP proposals: they are being asked to marry them.

This is patently ridiculous. Why should corporate executives give anybody a blank check? And why Data Processing? There isn't much evidence to show that the DP group is somehow favored. Occasionally, the situation is quite the opposite.

The chief operating officer for a successful public opinion firm was livid at a meeting where executive commitment was discussed. He told me that he was sick and tired about hearing people from Data Processing lecture him about the need for commitment. He wanted to see some commitment from Data Processing! He wasn't getting the information he needed! Promised deliveries were late! There wasn't any training! There wasn't any support! Data Processing dumped those Personal Computers on his department and then they disappeared! His people had to invent ways around some of the problems they found in the systems! When DP asked for commitment, it acted like it was going down a one-way street! We could take our requests for executive commitment and …

He had a point. We had not considered our request for executive commitment from the executive's point of view. We were so certain of the nobleness of our intentions that we somehow assumed our senior management was obligated to support us. We weren't sure exactly how they were supposed to support us, other than to approve the proposed project budget, but we wanted solid support.

What Exactly Is Executive Commitment?

What we should have been looking for was executive participation. We needed a number of things in addition to money. As things eventually turned out, simple budget approval was probably the worst thing the executives could have done.

We could have started with some feedback as to whether the changes brought about by the new system would fit well with the executives' views of the direction of the business. We had concentrated on the technical issues. We developed some critical success factors, but they were issues like terminal response, and the replacement of user manuals by on-line HELP facilities. The technical details said little about the changes to the business.

We had defined the new system in order to solve current system problems. This is not uncommon. Users understand problems because they are having them now or can predict their appearance in the near future. The users tell the systems group about the problems and the systems group responds by doing what systems groups do—it makes plans to change the current system or to build a new one as a replacement. As the saying goes, "When all you have is a hammer, every problem looks like a nail."

Executives understand problems in a different light. They are called upon to deal with issues that can't be resolved at lower levels of the enterprise. They also consider the need to move the enterprise forward. One of the key roles for executive management is the setting of directions and goals for the enterprise. The Data Processing group needs to understand those goals and directions and needs to be prepared to show how its work is directly supporting them.

Executive participation would have helped us to better understand some of the factors that might require us to make future changes in the system. The enterprise reacts to outside events and there are usually several scenarios that executive management considers.

To the executive managers it makes no sense to plunge into the refinement of current systems if there are going to be new requirements generated by entirely new types of business activity. Perhaps mergers or purchases are on the horizon that will bring the desirable systems technology in-house without internal development.

This is a tricky area for the executives and the Data Processing group. The executives of the ABC corporation don't want their DP staff gossiping about plans to take over XYZ, Inc. In a situation like this, the executives may choose to place relative emphasis on certain information systems activities that they feel might compliment the acquisition.

This can confuse and upset the DP staff, who may feel that the executives simply don't understand the current problems. So be it. The DP staff does not make company policy. However, the managers in the Data Processing group need to make it clear to executive management that the concept of "need to know" should extend far enough to allow DP to be prepared to support new corporate initiatives, even if all the details can't be revealed. There are very few corporate initiatives that would not benefit from well-organized and available data.

Executive participation is needed to establish the criteria for measuring DP success. There will seldom be a situation where Data Processing is measured solely by its own internal standards. Company executives will be concerned with measuring performance and financial impact at the business level, not at the system level.

This is very important. It acts to join the interests of Data Processing and the system users. Executive participation in establishing business goals makes it clear that all parties have a stake in the success of the systems development or enhancement effort. It acts to eliminate finger-pointing before it starts.

Executive participation is necessary for adjudication when the need to split resources between several projects means that some form of triage is necessary. The Data Processing group should not make unilateral decisions to cut back or re-schedule work that has been scheduled and budgeted. The concurrence of either the affected user, or the approval of executive management is needed. The Data Processing group is seldom in the best position to understand all the business ramifications of such decisions.

Executive participation is also needed for regular reviews of project progress. There is usually little to do at these reviews if the project is following the plan which was laid out for it, but such reviews serve the useful purpose of reassuring all parties—executives, Data Processing personnel, and system users—that the goals of the project remain valid and that the expected benefits remain intact.

There Are Some Real Problems Too

Everything said so far about executive participation is good, as far as it goes. It also needs to be said that things are sometimes much more difficult in practice. Corporate politics and personality clashes in the executive ranks are real, they are not as uncommon as most of us would like them to be, and they can exert a strong influence on information systems projects and funding.

There is no magic formula that will ensure rational systems planning in the face of irrationality at the executive level. The best approach in this situation is to try to insert some additional factors into the process, if only to keep one's own sanity.

Data Processing managers have a pretty good idea about the relative value of the things that DP is asked to do. If the DP group is continually forced to take actions which they don't feel are in the best interests of the company, or if technical constraints force them to develop too many "kludges" (software that the author would be embarrassed to show to her peers), the result will be burnout and rapid personnel turnover in the DP staff.

Be judicious in choosing additional factors to introduce into an already irrational systems planning process. Many arguments cut both ways. An argument that the Open Systems approach is the only general strategy to ensure long-term systems independence can come back to haunt you if you later need to argue for a process-specific system that uses proprietary architecture.

Somewhat better is the, "After that, then what?" approach. Short-term planning horizons often have substantial longer term costs, and the longer term is seldom far away. The choice of a "quick and dirty fix" instead of a longer-term, more expensive re-development does not eliminate the need for the longer-term project, it simply postpones it. There are usually some measurable and substantial costs involved, and, if they are brought into the open as part of the planning process, they can act as a brake on runaway executive opinions.

In situations where an attempt is made to bring greater rationality to the systems planning process, DP managers who have some understanding of finance will find the going much easier. It is not difficult to learn how to calculate the Net Present Value of a proposed systems development project and the DP manager should be able to both do this as well as discuss it with the people in corporate finance.

Some of the inputs to the financial valuation of proposed systems work are going to be soft. There's not much that the Data Processing manager will be able to do about it. The best thing to do is to remember Gilb's Law, "There is always a way to measure something which is better than not measuring it at all."

Armed with a financial yardstick the DP manager can propose a plan of action. At this point she can request that the executives review her plan and make any modifications required for non-financial reasons. If the financials have been developed with the help of the financial staff, the "where did you come up with these numbers?" issue can be quickly put to rest.

There is no guarantee that this approach will get action. Particularly in situations where personality conflicts are present in the executive ranks, the Data Processing manager can find herself called on to simultaneously satisfy multiple conflicting agendas. The best thing to do in this situation is to do nothing. Gather the agendas together, make sure each party to the dispute has all the information that you do, and ask for a business decision. When your users complain about non-responsiveness (and they will complain), give them the same material you gave the executives and tell them where to take their complaints. Eventually, the pain will grow great enough that the logjam will be broken. Eventually may mean months or years: Weeks are seldom enough.

You can suggest that an independent third party, such as a well-known consulting firm, be brought in to assist with systems planning. It's surprising how often executives go along with this approach. The biggest problem in adopting this course of action is that the needed executive participation may be replaced by consultant participation, which is not the same by any stretch of the imagination.

Executive participation really *is* needed by the Data Processing group. Information is essential to the operation of the enterprise, and the quality of the information is a key to effective management at both the operational and executive levels. The time and attention of corporate executives can be difficult to get, but the DP managers should be persistent in demanding a share of that time for the good of the enterprise as a whole.

If the share of time is forthcoming, the DP managers must be prepared to give as well as get. They owe the executives a clear explanation of the issues where executive guidance is sought. They need to be prepared to provide educational presentations in order to supply background information and context related to those matters which have technical content.

If Data Processing wants to have executive commitment it will be far better if the commitment is in the form of a regular forum rather than in blind approval for the project of the moment. Data Processing staffs know that the process of repenting for hasty systems decisions is hardly ever leisurely.

7

Enterprise Funding

For years, people have commented on the fragmentation of information held in company computers and the incompatibility of the systems that access this data. The need for overall corporate systems planning has been stated in many forums. Some companies have created the post of Chief Information Officer, giving that person a broad mandate to bring order out of chaos in the world of systems.

Chaos remains thoroughly entrenched.

It is going to remain with us until companies restructure the way in which funding is allocated for information services. At present the dominant approach is a sort of auction where individuals and groups within the corporation (including the Data Processing group itself) compete to get *their* systems work done. Each system sponsor will develop arguments as to the low cost, low risk, and enormous benefits of the system they are proposing. The arguments will be passed on for review under the budget process. This is the corporate version of the politician's smoke-filled room.

It is only in the rarest of cases that the process of selecting systems projects is based on a genuine understanding of the likely impacts to the enterprise. Several times I have seen multi-phase system development proposals emerge with funding approval for only the first and last phases.

This is not altogether the fault of the people assembling the budgets. They are bombarded by independent proposals, not only for systems, but for other corporate projects (such as the establishment of day-care centers). The job is like trying to read a novel using a strobe light for illumination. Everyone is trying to capture their attention by focusing on a specific issue.

It is not easy to consider the long-term corporate good when your career prospects depend on short-term performance. If the plant manager in Des Moines feels he needs enhancements to the order tracking system, he will not want to hear a lecture about the need for a uniform approach to part numbering. His job performance is measured by how well the Des Moines plant functions. The plant manager will go up the executive chain demanding at each step that something be done to help him out. Eventually, he may receive a budget variance to pay for the work he wants.

It is in such a fashion that systems grow. About eighty percent of the functionality of today's mature systems was added after the development phase had been completed. Virtually none of this growth has been coordinated under a plan that considers the overall information assets of the enterprise.

A Tool for Change

In his recent book,[1] J. Alfred French provides a good sketch of the current systems landscape:

> *"Duplication, redundancy and re-implementation of separate application-oriented systems continue to fragment thinking and information. Global information opportunities go unnoticed in the surge to maintain, fix, or enhance a part here or a part there.*
>
> *Thousands of Toms, Joes and Debbies are spending hours of computer time developing tidbits of data, most of which will never be used to produce one cent of profit. Almost everyone in business is scanning or toting thousands of lines of video screens or spreadsheets that should never have been produced."*

1. J. Alfred French, *The Business Knowledge Investment*, (Prentice Hall, 1990). This book is an excellent introduction to the issues encountered in developing enterprise information architectures.

It's clear that something must change. It's also clear that the systems group does not have the leverage to force changes in the way funding is allocated throughout the corporation. This does not mean that the current situation can't be improved. It is possible to move toward coordinated systems planning. It is important to the enterprise that this be done.

In the first place, coordinated systems planning can reduce both the time and cost required to change systems in response to changes in business requirements. In the second place, coordinated systems planning can be a proactive force—enabling the enterprise to improve levels of service, anticipate changes in the marketplace, and increase job satisfaction. The result of an improved, coordinated planning process can be a strategic advantage for the enterprise.

One of the major obstacles to coordination is the lack of an accepted reference point. What are the information assets? How are they distributed? How can the organizational impacts of system and information changes be identified and tracked? Several companies are turning to the development of an *enterprise model* in order to provide the needed information.

Enterprise models have a long and undistinguished career. Typically, they have been developed by the systems organization as a tool to facilitate long-term systems planning. During the development of the model, there is (sometimes) extensive contact with system users and corporate executives. The model is completed, a strategic system plan dutifully follows, and soon the model falls into disuse and begins its slide toward irrelevance as systems funding resumes its familiar pattern.

This is a shame. Companies *need* tools like enterprise models to help them think about systems and their impacts. Data Processing departments need enterprise models to put their activities into perspective. It's important for both users and systems people to understand why there have been so many disappointments associated with enterprise modeling over the years.

Companies need to recognize that the enterprise model is not a thing, but a process. Although the data and relationships used to describe the enterprise have "thing-ness" about them, they can only represent the enterprise at a point in time. The enterprise is a living entity that changes continuously. This means that the data and relationships that constitute the knowledge base cannot be etched in stone.

The manner in which the enterprise model is created must focus on the process of change and on the way that change will affect the input, content, and usage of the knowledge base. A model that will forever tell you how your company worked on December 15, 1990 will be of limited use.

Those charged with developing the enterprise model need to address the information gathering process and the information representation mechanism. These are the drivers of the enterprise model. The technical structure of the knowledge base is a secondary issue. The information representation mechanism—the way that the knowledge base is presented to the users—is what is usually considered when modeling is discussed.

The Model and Its Users

In order to be useful the enterprise model must serve the needs of groups with different viewpoints. The operations division sees a customer location as a point of reference for a unit that needs to be installed or repaired. To marketing, it's part of a demographic area. To sales, it's used for account management and commission calculations. To finance, it determines which taxing authority is involved. Changes in the information associated with a customer location will affect operations, marketing, finance and sales. The changes will be viewed by these divisions in different ways. The enterprise model must be able to present information about changes to the way that customer location data is defined and accessed in a format that will be useful to each of the affected divisions.

This is not a case where one size fits all. The search for a single presentation form that will effectively communicate to a variety of groups will probably be futile. However, recently developed tools may make it possible to develop models that support multiple presentation formats while relating them to a common knowledge base.

Enterprise models are one area where use of hypertext and hypermedia tools should be very effective. The ability to set up user-defined presentation and browsing mechanisms will increase the usage of the knowledge base, and usage is critical to the success of the enterprise model.

Groups within the company should refer to the enterprise model as a matter of course during their planning process and operational reviews. For this to happen, the people who use the model must convince themselves that it really helps them do their jobs. If use of the model forces people to deal with representations or terminology that are unnatural to them, they will never realize its potential.

Not only are there different fundamental views reflecting the interest of the groups using the enterprise model's knowledge base, there are different representations within each group, depending upon the level at which the information is presented. The VP for customer services needs a different level of information than his operations manager. The basic mechanism of hypertext, which supports a user-defined hierarchy for the presentation and linkage of information, looks like a promising technology to handle the wide range of representation requirements.

Ownership of the Model

When considering enterprise modeling as a process, it's necessary for the users to be actively involved. Active involvement is the only way of ensuring that the knowledge base remains current. In most corporations there is no single department or person who can supply the level of detail that needs to be represented by the enterprise model. Because of this, the enterprise modeling effort needs to consider the advantages of a distributed ownership of the knowledge base representations.

A distributed ownership of the representations means that each group will have the ability to change the way the enterprise information is presented, thus helping it to best serve their purposes. The group that integrates the elements of the enterprise model needs to make allowances for supporting users in making these changes.

This user ownership of part of the enterprise model is a key to the other major element of the enterprise modeling process—knowledge acquisition. As planning and operational environments change, different groups will use different information. By introducing new elements into the model as part of their representation, the group or division who uses them will bring the new elements to the attention of the group responsible for knowledge base maintenance. At that point the knowledge base maintenance group can perform the necessary analysis to establish the linkages with other groups.

The formation of a knowledge base maintenance group is an issue which is bypassed by modeling methodologies that envision the model as a *thing* to be produced. It is only when the enterprise model is viewed as a *process* that the importance of maintenance becomes evident. The maintenance group has the responsibility of ensuring that the user group representations are both accurate and complete. The members of the maintenance group are responsible for training and supporting the users in the actual use of the model. They are the ones who are responsible for providing the terminology translations between the user groups.

Although the enterprise modeling maintenance group will probably be part of the Data Processing organization, it must be free to function as an independent entity. This group should not be required to satisfy the needs of systems planning alone. If the model is regarded as being focused strictly on data processing systems planning and not encompassing operational and organizational views, it will fall into disuse.

The enterprise model is a planning tool and, of all the planning tools available, it has the best chance of improving the rationality of the project selection process. At the point where changes to the existing systems environment are first suggested, the systems and user organizations should turn immediately to the enterprise model. It can help both groups to work in partnership in order to understand clearly the impacts on corporate information.

This understanding is critical to coordinated systems planning. In the same way that the enterprise model can improve communications between the systems group and the systems sponsor, it can also improve communication with other groups in the enterprise who will be affected by the changes under consideration. The use of a good enterprise model can be very beneficial in JAD sessions. It can reduce the time required from the participants, and it can establish a common reference point for discussing requirements and impacts.

The combination of JAD sessions and the enterprise model allows the systems organization to take a proactive role in the funding process. The systems director can draw up a budget based on a consensus of the way that will best allocate systems resources for the benefit of the enterprise as a whole. The effects of external constraints, such as executive directives to reduce all budget requests by fifteen percent, can be quickly evaluated and either accommodated or appealed.

An interesting side effect of using an enterprise model is that it can accelerate systems funding approvals. It does this by demonstrating the role of existing assets in proposed projects. A proposal to use information that is already available will almost never be regarded as having the same risk level as a project that starts out needing new sources of data. Even if the entirely new system poses less risk than one which uses current assets, there will always be an initial bias to believe that "new" equals "risk" and "existing" equals "sure thing."

By fostering cooperative consideration of systems development by system technicians and system users, the enterprise model can serve as an impetus to funding process improvement. In fact, it is the cooperation rather than the model that brings rationality to project selection. The model serves as a catalyst. It is not a panacea for the problems of providing effective systems for the enterprise, and it is not as simple as drawing up a set of diagrams. The systems people involved with developing and maintaining the enterprise model will need negotiating skills in addition to technical ability.

It is naive to believe that everyone will buy into the cooperative systems development process. It is likewise naive to believe that systems funding decisions will become totally rational. What enterprise modelling does is give the enterprise a better chance of making the right systems development and enhancement choices. It is the responsibility of those managing systems groups to ensure that the enterprise has that better chance.

8

The Only Two Measures That Count

How good is your Data Processing operation? Are you doing better this year than last year? Do you know where improvement is possible? Do you know how much improvement is possible? Are you worried that your group is being left behind as technology advances? Are you worried that you don't always know what your own organization is doing?

Calm yourself. You can simplify your life if you remember that there are only two things that determine how good the Data Processing operation is. You can identify them, quantify them and measure them. Everyone in your department will understand them, and your users will too.

The first is data quality. The second is information access.

Without data quality, there can be no information asset to manage. Incorrect data, missing data, conflicting data, out-of-date data, useless data—the more of these you have, the more trouble you're in. Your programs might run perfectly. Your programmers may achieve spectacular levels of productivity. Your interfaces may be the most user-friendly in the business. But if all of this excellence in technology is regurgitating bad data, you're probably hurting your company rather than helping it.

It doesn't take much bad data to hurt you. A sign I saw on a Quality Assurance manager's desk sums it up:

> *One barrel of sewage plus one cup of wine equals one barrel of sewage.*
>
> *One barrel of wine plus one cup of sewage equals one barrel of sewage.*

As your users realize that they can't rely on the output they get from your systems, the value of the information asset you are responsible for will diminish rapidly. People will start to get their data from other sources. They'll keep their own data on their PC's. You won't know what's there. You can't make it available to other people who might need it. You won't know if it is better or worse than the data you already have.

Like crabgrass, bad data springs up in unexpected places. There's seldom just one patch of it. It takes a lot of effort to get rid of it. It can really mess up your lawn. The problem is that bad data is used by people when they make decisions and decisions based on bad data can adversely affect the enterprise. Bad sales data can lead to production schedules that are too ambitious, causing too much raw material to be ordered. Use of bad data can lead to large stocks of finished goods sitting in warehouses, and substantial interest charges on money borrowed to support unnecessary production.

If the sales manager chooses to use data kept on his own personal computer because he feels he can't rely on the sales data he gets from Data Processing, there's a good chance that the problems will never be corrected. What will *that* mean for the company?

It won't do you any good to complain that the errors in the Data Processing data are caused by the bad input you get from the office in Buzzard Flats. You are the one responsible for the information asset. Get down to Buzzard Flats and find out how you can work with the people there to solve your problem. It really is *your* problem. Your users are complaining about the data they are getting from *your* system, aren't they?

Everyone has heard the statement that "Garbage In Equals Garbage Out." This is untrue! Garbage Out is *greater* than Garbage In. Garbage In data, if recognized, can simply be fixed. Garbage Out data will influence decisions and courses of action that can require monumental efforts to correct. And all during the correction process, people are going to remember that they got the Garbage Out data from the systems you're responsible for.

Making sure the data is accurate is not a trivial task. The best place to start is at the point of data entry. It is less expensive, by an order of magnitude, to prevent bad data from entering your systems than it is to locate it and correct it once it's there.

Become familiar with the order entry process, the sales transaction process, the shipping and distribution process, and all the other processes where data comes in from the outside world to be stored in your systems. Check to see that the customer service representative works with the customer to make sure that the name and address are correct. Check to see if part numbers have check digits included in them so that transpositions of characters can be spotted. If you notice places where improvements can be made, take the initiative to suggest them.

Look beyond the field layout on the screens. Look at the data entry operation as a whole. Are the operators trained? Is the work area comfortable and well-lit? How is work distribution handled? Are the documents which come in from internal sources or suppliers filled out legibly? Find out how operator performance is measured and rewarded. It all makes a difference to what is going into your systems, no matter how far it is physically from the computer room.

Look carefully at situations where data is keyed in from computer-generated forms. Are your data entry operators expected to figure out the ghostly digits on the back copy of a six-part form? Are they asked to enter long strings of digits? Are the fields on the form separated to allow the data to be clearly identified? If you make things difficult for the people who put data into the system, they will, however unintentionally, make things difficult for you.

Don't forget to check to see if you're collecting the right data. If you're collecting information on automobile repairs through a system that requires detailed model and body type breakdowns for American cars but not for foreign cars, the ability of users to draw meaningful inferences from the data you collected will be constrained. It may be that nobody uses the detailed American car information any more, but the company is still paying for collecting it. You need to be sure that the data you have is relevant as well as accurate.

Look at the edits to incoming data provided by your systems. Are they complete? Do they make sense? Learn about the problems they are supposed to solve. Keep a log of the special actions needed to clean up problem data. Look for patterns that indicate underlying problems.

Check to be sure that the means for correcting errors are not providing the opportunity to make other errors. It is not unusual to have sophisticated error detection logic combined with error correction procedures which rely entirely on the accuracy of the human operator. While it is true that every operation needs to have utilities available that can operate directly on data with few, if any, restrictions; use of these tools must not become a common practice.

Look out for multiple copies of the same data. There are few events more confusing than meetings where there are two different sets of numbers which supposedly came from the same source. But this is exactly what can happen if there are multiple copies of data with no plan to keep them coordinated.

Beware of multiple update paths. If something goes wrong, it may be tough to find out where the problem is. Data sharing across systems raises the odds that there will be multiple updates—particularly as functionality moves from one system to another. Process changes that involve multiple systems changes and migrations can be sources of errors that are very difficult to identify and isolate.

Consider creating an independent audit function for your data. As your databases expand in size and complexity, it may be difficult to insure that new programs have all the correct data edits or that older edits are brought up to current standards. An independent program can examine a sample of your data in such a way that you will have a statistically significant indication if anything is wrong. The assistance of a good statistician can help you to keep the sample size down and help you to understand the results.

Think about how much of your data comes from outside sources. There are market analysis services, industry surveys, component specifications, shipping schedules, phone bills—all sorts of useful data. If you want your Data Processing contribution to the enterprise to provide a maximum contribution, you need to consider the accuracy of the outside data as well as that of the data that you collect internally. Outside and inside data are typically combined in business processes and, since a chain is no stronger than its weakest link, a process may be limited by the quality of the outside data it uses.

If your enterprise is getting inaccurate data from outside sources, get involved! You wouldn't be quiet if you purchased software that didn't work. If you plan to take a leadership role in defining and managing the information asset of your organization, you need to be involved in ensuring that all the data is accurate, not just yours.

As you are making your data more accurate, don't forget that you also need to make it accessible. Accurate data that nobody can obtain is not par-

ticularly valuable. Until it comes out of your systems in a form that somebody can use to guide his or her actions, it isn't information at all.

> *"Imagine a huge library run by a maniacal reference clerk. The
> library is loaded with valuable information, but half the card cata-
> logue is missing, and you must conduct your search by flashlight."*
>   Paul Saffo

Access to data means that your users can get at the data they need when
they need it. This doesn't have to be a complex, query-oriented environment.
It may be as simple as getting a two-page report on a manager's desk by 8:30
each morning. But you do need to put the right information on those two
pages.

Accessibility means more than computers and systems that are up and
on-line twenty-four hours a day. It does the user no good at all to get wel-
come screens and menus that give her many choices—but not the ones she
really needs. Access means that your users can get the data they need in a
form they can use. A manager who needs to know the number of rebuilt carburetors shipped last week doesn't want to get this information from a big
report that shows the number of carburetors shipped to each sales region and
sub-region. She just wants a number, preferably in a setting where it's clear
that the number relates to carburetor shipments.

There is a time value to data, and many users are very sensitive to it.
Would anyone buy *The Wall Street Journal* if its most recent stock listings
were three days old? The availability and timeliness of data have a major
effect on the business processes that the data supports. Work with your users
to understand their business process. Ask what would happen if they could
get up-to-date data on demand. Find out what would happen if the data they
used was updated twice a day instead of every other day.

Look at the time value of data from the cost aspect as well. Keeping
data updated on a real-time basis costs more than updating it periodically
and printing a report which is then given to the user for her reference. Work
with your users so that they understand the trade-offs that are involved. Try
to define what the real needs are so that the timeliness requirements for data
can be satisfied.

Accessibility of information is defined by users who need to access it,
not by Data Processing managers or database architects. The needs for
access are constantly changing and the ability of your department to respond
to these changes is a very good measure of how good your department is.

Find out what your users want to do with the information they get. Several times I've found that users are making do with marginal data because

they don't know that more useful information is available. Find out if data shipped to one department is being passed to another department who is using it second-hand. Find out if this is occurring because of barriers that Data Processing has built up over the years.

I met recently with some managers from a reference services organization within a large manufacturing and service company. It seemed that while they had some internal customers who would rather lay off staff than cut back on reference services, other internal customers were discouraging staff use of the available reference services, preferring in some cases to obtain these services from outside firms. The amazing thing (at least to me) was that the reference service managers had no idea how the information they supplied was used by their customers. They had no idea how the company benefitted from their activities. They did not know why some of their customers now used outside firms. Furthermore, they had no plans to find these things out.

This is lunacy. If an organization is responsible for delivering correct data in a timely manner, there is no way they can judge their own effectiveness without understanding what is being done with the data they supply. Instead of decrying the inadequacy of communications with their users, the organization's managers have a golden opportunity to be proactive in aligning their work with the processes of their customers. This is true for reference services, Data Processing, or any other information provider.

Make sure your users understand that you're serious when you ask if they're receiving the information they need when they need it. If there are problems, act on them. By tracking the types of problems and their solutions, you will have a good indication of the degree to which your department is improving.

If you really concentrate on data quality and information access, your department's performance will improve to the point where your users will start to take excellence for granted.

But that's a problem of a different sort.

9

The Elusive Nature of Information

What we do is Data Processing. We understand the mechanics of data. We describe it, we model it, we process it, we report it. Information is more difficult to grasp. We can begin to describe how information is born—someone receives data, they recognize that they have received it, they put it into context, and they use the combination of data and context to influence an action. Data has become information.

The relationship between data and information remains maddeningly difficult to quantify. It usually implies an exchange—it is brought into being by a stimulus and a response. Claude Shannon's work[1] provides a basis for thinking about the capacity of data to convey information. But information content in these terms is inadequate to gauge the value of the signal which is received. Shannon himself recognized this problem and stated his clear intention to deal strictly with the engineering aspects of communication.

1. For a superb overview of Shannon's contribution, read Robert W. Lucky's book, *Silicon Dreams,* (St. Martins Press, 1989).

We may be faced with a problem similar to that of quantifying art. Van Gogh, Monet, and Wyeth have all painted flowers, but each painting is different in obvious ways. If we describe all the physical ways in which they differ, we will still lack an understanding of how each can call forth a different response from the visitor in the gallery.

Information in the enterprise resembles art in that it triggers a response. In many cases, perhaps the majority, the response is to try to obtain more information—"Production has dropped by 3%; let me see the re-work figures." One day in 1977, the Maryland lottery operations staff began to see thousands of bets on the number 463. A quick check showed that there had been no widely publicized events with that number—for example, Flight 463 had not been hijacked. There was concern that the bets were a manifestation of a system error. All the external indicators pointed to a normally functioning system. All the data available was not sufficient to create the desired information. The decision to keep the system going was made in a situation where it wasn't clear what was really going on.[2] The existing data was not conclusive, but it was not clear what sort of data would be needed.

This is a common occurrence. There are very few situations where the decision maker has complete data about the situation at the point where a decision must be made. Even if all the relevant data is available, the information it yields can lead to incorrect actions. The grandmasters of chess can see the whole board. They have all the data in front of them. They have a wealth of knowledge about previous games similar to the one they are playing. But games are still won and lost through mistakes.

The accuracy (in a physical sense) of the data crossing the interface between system and user is not enough to ensure that information transfer has taken place; at least when human beings are involved. When passing data between computers or from a computer to a mechanical or electrical device, we pronounce the interface to be correct when our tests show that it reliably supports the physical exchange. There are those who would argue that what is being passed in this instance is, indeed, information. The data has a context and causes an action.

I'm not comfortable with an argument at this level. To my way of thinking, an important characteristic of the relationship between data and information is the degree to which it is indeterminate. We really don't understand

---

2. What had actually happened is that the previous evening's episode of a popular television show portrayed the leading character as making a numbers bet that won. The number was 463.

the mechanism of transfer. How is it that a seemingly innocuous item of data can trigger an important insight into the nature of a process?

Information has a time element in addition to a content element. After the race is run we know which horse finished first. If we had known that fact earlier, it could have been used as information and, in a very practical way, we might be richer for knowing it. Furthermore, the time element is related to the sequence in which data is received. Time, sequence, and content act together to provide a context into which further data is received. As the context becomes richer, we say that we know about the subjects that the data describes.

By stating that we know something, we are saying that we have organized our data so that it can be readily converted to information. In Data Processing, we see continually how important it is to present data in the proper form. Why are there so many requests for format changes in reports and screens? It's because the current screens do not reinforce the user's knowledge or learning pattern. The data may be there, but it isn't becoming information.

Those of us who work with Data Processing systems have a responsibility to do the best job we can to present data so that it can be converted into information and knowledge. Increasingly, this means that we need to emphasize tools that allow the people who use our systems to have a direct say in gathering the data which they use.

Up to this point, the Data Processing business has concentrated on presenting the data itself. It is only with the advent of the personal computer that we can see the potential for providing tools as well. What has the advent of PC-based spreadsheet programs done for the use of quantitative data in management? Plenty. It has allowed users to organize data so that it matches the context in which it will be converted to information. The emerging Hypertext environments are pointing the way to similar advances in the handling of loosely-coupled data, such as text.

On the frontiers of research, initiatives like Ted Nelson's Project Xanadu and Apple's Knowledge Navigator provide descriptions of what the world of information could become. Such portrayals are meant to challenge our current assumptions about the way that humans, computers, communications and information will work together. People who have seen Apple's Knowledge Navigator video or similar material produced by DEC, HP or AT&T are often initially skeptical because they have become conditioned to react to data as it is presented today. We are unsteady when asked to define new, more effective ways of obtaining data. Ironically, we often feel we need more data before we can answer this question.

Over the next two decades we should expect to see an explosive growth in end-user computing. Fueled by the rapid growth of personal computing, increasingly sophisticated and powerful tools have become widely available. Users have applied these tools to build systems tailored to their needs. It is through end-user computing that we will be able to realize a significant improvement in the use of quantitative information in our enterprises. The manner in which this use of quantitative data changes work and society is a subject that will keep futurists fully engaged for many years.

Many practical issues in enterprises today revolve around the relationship between data and information. The design and execution of effective Executive Information Systems is one of these. The development and change of powerful, personalized data browsers is a complex task, made more so by the need to respond quickly to requests for data at the executive level. In this situation the system must act to help the user find the data needed so that information that supports decisions can be developed. There is a wide variety of data and a wide variety of decisions that must be supported.

A factor that makes the task appear even more complex is our predisposition to think of data within the context of a process which uses it. It is difficult for many of us to visualize multiple processes using data concurrently. It's also hard to evaluate the linkages between the processes as they change in reaction to the data as it becomes available. However, it is this multitude of processes and their interaction that is the norm in environments which rely on the identification and use of information.

It's interesting to speculate on whether the difficulty of building computer systems is related to the underlying difficulties in relating data and information. We build systems out of a wonderfully malleable material—pure thought stuff—but we have trouble creating structures which hold their shape. The target always seems out of reach when we try to build systems for others to use.

One factor that causes problems is the lack of tools that represent information as well as data. How can we represent an information value that depends upon timeliness, context, and content? Does the fact that today's software engineering tools can only handle the quantitative aspects of data constrain our ability to think about the underlying information? Good questions. I wonder what the answers will look like.

One thing is becoming obvious, however. The structured design and information engineering approaches to building computer systems can only take us so far. They artificially restrict us to things that are relatively easy to measure and relatively easy to manipulate. We need a way to go beyond these constraints. We need to understand how the data we manage is turned into information as it is used in the processes it supports. We need to under-stand the real information needs of the processes and of the people who manage them.

The Dark Side of the Data

Our thinking processes are shaped by the tools we use to help us think. The ability of a personal computer to deliver not only data but also the power to manipulate it, has changed the way that data is used and regarded. All too often, there is an inclination to work within the limits established by the tools. The consequence is that information that cannot be easily obtained or manipulated is ignored.

Placing an incorrect value in a spreadsheet cell does not make it cor-rect. We have all seen banks fold and lives get ruined although the numbers looked fine. A smoothly running simulation does not produce a tangible product, while a jury-rigged production process often does.

Management is the art of understanding both the quantitative measures and the qualitative forces that lie behind them. To the extent that a fascina-tion with manipulation of the tools and data diminishes the attention paid to the critical issue of what the data represents, the business processes sup-ported by the data are likely to work less well than they did before.

Beyond this is the issue of our expectations as we work with data and the technology that is available to manipulate it. If we become uncomfort-able with data that takes a long time to develop or collect, we may find our-selves avoiding its use. As more and more concentration is placed on data that can be made available quickly and less use is made of data from sources that force us to wait, the stability of our enterprises may be subtly under-mined. Companies whose operating strategies are guided by quarterly oper-ating results or changes in stock price seem to have great difficulty in establishing or maintaining a base for sustained growth.

When we look at Japanese companies, we should notice two things. The first is that computer usage for management support is not nearly as widespread in Japan as it is in the United States. The second is that the importance of the data used in supporting management decision making is not tied to the ease with which it can be manipulated to make nice graphs or "fearless projections du Jour."

In successful Japanese companies, management and the use of data are inextricably joined. One difference is often noted as critical by writers deal-ing with Japanese management. It is the manner in which the Japanese manager cares for the value and timeliness of the data that he uses and for which he is responsible.

I do not believe it is possible to develop a long-term strategic view of an enterprise if one feels compelled to use technology to get quick answers. Quick answers are, by necessity, based on a web of assumptions. Assumptions are no substitute for data obtained through empirical means. To the extent that our marvelous machines are allowed to supplant empirical data, our enterprises are sure to suffer the consequences.

10

The Analyst's Masquerade

Really big project failures always start with a failure of analysis. No matter how good the programming, no matter how advanced the computers, no matter how substantial the funding, errors made in analysis will doom the project. The failure will be announced by the user, who says, "The system doesn't do what I need."

Analysis is the part of the Data Processing function where alchemy is still practiced. Because each analysis is unique, it is the hardest activity to explain and evaluate. It's also a time bomb. Failures in analysis are particularly dangerous because they reappear later in the systems development process.

When the failures reappear, the consequence is often a frantic effort to "get around" the system constraints that came from the original analysis. The word most often used to describe the results is "kludge" (pronounced "klooj")—an undocumented, ill-arranged combination of software and/or hardware that has been thrown together to provide at least some functionality, and which will be the cause of severe mental stress for the people who have to maintain it.

Although it is widely understood that the cost of correcting system problems rises the farther one moves past the analysis stage, kludges are taken for granted in the Data Processing business. In some cases, they are considered as a source of pride by those who put them together. This casual acceptance of the failure of analysis is a damning indictment of Data Processing's pretensions of professionalism.

Even worse, as an industry Data Processing doesn't seem to care about the root cause of poor analysis. Errors in analysis are regarded as being part of the normal order of things, much like bugs in programs.

Where Bad Analysis Comes From

The fact is that there are very few things that the Data Processing business does worse than developing good analysts. Almost without exception, an analyst is someone who began as a programmer and moved up the ladder through promotion. The idea that systems analysis is not simply a natural extension to programming is foreign to most Data Processing managers.

Analysis differs from programming in much the same way that poker differs from chess. In programming (chess), all of the required information is available. The programmer has complete control over the instructions the computer will execute just as the chess player has complete control over the pieces he moves. Just as there is no theoretical reason that makes it impossible to play a perfect game of chess, there is no theoretical barrier to writing a program that contains no technical errors.[1]

In analysis (poker), the situation is different. Information is not out in the open. The analyst needs to figure out what the system needs to do just as the poker player needs to figure out whether his cards are better than his opponents'. Communication about the true state of things is imperfect. The analyst needs to work with the user and the poker player needs to study his opposition. If either the poker player or the analyst makes a mistake, money will be lost.

Despite the fundamental difference between programming and analysis, there is virtually no training provided to insure that the analyst can do his job the way it needs to be done. In part this is because the ability to perform

---

1. There is no *practical* barrier to writing error-free programs, either. Harlan Mills taught a programming course where the students were expected to write a non-trivial program that ran correctly the first time it was executed. The course was graded as pass/fail and the program counted for 100% of the grade. The majority of students passed the course.

good analysis is still regarded as a gift—some people are good at it and some people never will be.

What Analysts Do

There are a number of misconceptions about analysis. Perhaps the most prevalent is that analysis is primarily a solitary, cerebral activity. Most analysts believe this out of self-interest. The creative aspects of analysis can provide great personal satisfaction. However, creativity that gives satisfaction to the individual is not guaranteed to give equivalent satisfaction to the enterprise.

Analysis cannot exist in a vacuum; it requires effective communication. There must be effective communication with the users who will be served by the system under consideration. There must be effective communication with those who will provide resources so that the system can be developed. There must be effective communication with the people who will build the system so that they can understand what they need to do.

The analyst needs to communicate because he is expected to have his feet on two shores. He provides a translating function between user expectations and technical directives. He is expected to help the user identify the functionality that is needed to support the user's business processes, and he is expected to be able to describe this functionality in such a way that the technical staff can build a system to supply it. The analyst adds value to the work he does through his ability to bring imagination and creativity to the task, but the task he is performing is based on the requirement that he communicate effectively.

Recognizing the essential role of communication in analysis, some companies have set up teams made up of Business System Analysts and Computer System Analysts. The two are expected to work closely together to insure that both the business and technical aspects are covered by experts. In many cases, this approach has not worked as well as expected.

The practice of developing analysis teams made up of specialists needs to be carefully thought out before it is put into practice. It can have the effect of adding additional distortion to the communication between users and the people who are developing or enhancing systems. The result can be much like the game we played as children where one person whispers a message to the next. The difference between the original message and the one the last player heard can be the source of considerable amusement (or embarrassment).

Furthermore, in any attempt to perform analysis using a group of specialists, the result is dependent upon the skills and attitudes of each of the specialists. The observation about the relationship of weak links and the strength of chains is absolutely true when applied to analysis teams. If analysis teams are to be effective, the enterprise must first ensure that its individual analysts are effective.

Basic Training for Analysts

Using combinations of specialists will not substitute for the proper training of analysts. This training should include both basic skills training and task-specific training. Many enterprises do not allow for either.

Basic skills training includes training in listening, public speaking, written and verbal communications, organizing and running meetings, estimating, and sales techniques. Of these, the most important is listening.

Effective listening can be taught. It's part of the basic training for psychologists, sociologists, and other professions where the nature of the work demands extensive interaction between human beings. If the analyst can't listen effectively, he can't ask effective questions and he will probably go forward with a number of misconceptions about the nature of the work to be done. Effective listening is not only necessary in dealing with the user, it is also necessary when dealing with the people who will be building or enhancing the system. The analyst needs to gauge the understanding of the technical team by paying attention to their comments and questions in response to what he tells them about the user's needs.

At some point the analyst will need to present the results of his analysis to both the users and to those who will implement his ideas. The abilities to speak both in public and in one-on-one settings, and to write with clarity are essential if the vision of the analyst is to be followed.   If the vision can't be communicated, the analysis might as well not be performed.

The analyst will spend a great deal of time in meetings. This is not often considered one of the fun parts of the job. There are, however, proven techniques that can make meetings both shorter and more effective. The analyst should be trained in these techniques and should encourage their use in the meetings he attends.

Analysts are regularly called upon to estimate the size, cost, and duration of systems development or enhancement efforts. However, it's rare that analysts are given formal training in estimating techniques or are encouraged to share estimating experiences with other analysts. As a consequence, most companies put little faith in the accuracy of system development estimates. It seems worthwhile to put some effort into improving the ability of analysts to provide accurate input to the funding and management process.

The suggestion that analysts should receive training in sales techniques seems curious at first. It's necessary to realize that one of the key jobs of the analyst is to sell the idea that the Data Processing group is capable of building a system to satisfy the user's needs. To do this requires not only that the Data Processing group develop a good product (the system development plan) but also that it obtain the user's confidence and support to actually implement the system.

Any user would like to hear analysts come back and say to them, "The system will do what you want it to do and it will cost much less than you expected it would, but you're going to have to live with the fact that it will be delivered well ahead of schedule." In real life there are trade-offs. Certain functionality might need to be delayed so that delivery of other functionality can take place in a timely manner. The cost of the system might be unacceptable without a change in user expectations. In all these situations the analyst is acting as a salesman or negotiator, trying to match the user's needs against the Data Processing organization's ability to satisfy them. For the good of the enterprise, it makes sense to ensure that analysts have the sales and negotiating skills to find a way through the jungle of trade-offs and occasional bruised egos.

Beyond the basic techniques, the analyst should receive training that is relevant to the work the system must do. This may involve taking some basic instruction in data entry or working in the shipping department for a few weeks. The analyst needs to have a base of experience to which he can relate the user's concerns. He also needs to make the user confident that he is able to speak the user's language. Direct experience in the user's operation is also helpful in developing contacts who can provide additional information as the work of analysis goes forward.

The basic training that an analyst should receive, particularly in effective listening, is the key to making his exposure to the user's operation worthwhile. The more information he can gather during this period, the better the chance that he will be able to add value to the overall effort through his own creativity.

In addition to this basic training, technical training of a more advanced nature may be required when dealing with new technologies or significant changes in the way that Data Processing supports the business processes. Detailed technical knowledge can be critical when realistic evaluations of feasibility are needed. Analysts whose detailed knowledge of technology is only a year or two old can be at a serious disadvantage in evaluating newer developments. That disadvantage can turn into disaster for the enterprise if it remains unacknowledged and uncorrected.

Effective training of analysts can start a positive cycle. Through an improved ability to do his job, the analyst can avoid mistakes. Since his training allows him to build a better understanding of what is to be done (and also the context in which the system is to function) he improves his chances for real creativity as he devises a system to meet the user's needs. The personal gratification which comes from the application of greater creativity and the resultant user satisfaction acts as a stimulus for further improvement.

An enterprise which helps its employees to effectively apply their intelligence and creativity to the problems of the business is going to prosper. It is the ability of the trained analyst to add value to the systems he is associated with that allows an enterprise to get the maximum value from the data it collects.

Typically, the analyst's job does not stop when the analysis is completed. The analyst lives with the project through its completion, providing additional clarification to developers, and negotiating any changes which are forced by business or technical factors. The analyst should take the lead in any post-implementation review, focusing on the degree to which the original analysis and its subsequent implementation actually did the job that needed to be done. Finally, the analyst needs to analyze his own performance.

It's at this point of review that the analyst may be able to see what went wrong and what went right. But without better training than analysts receive today, the analyst may not be able to improve his performance for the next project.

11

The Information Evangelist

Today, many Data Processing organizations are attempting to define and implement comprehensive subject databases which will be accessible throughout the enterprise. This is not an easy undertaking, but it makes a lot of sense as a second step.

What's the first step? The first step is to be sure that the enterprise is getting maximum value from the information it already has. Few enterprises are.

Most systems originated to serve specific needs for specific organizations within the enterprise. The data and associated functionality for the system were defined, the appropriate hardware complement to support the system was identified and, if necessary, purchased, and the system came to life. This happened because individual organizations took the time and effort to request that Data Processing build a system which did what they wanted it to, and because they were willing to put up budget money for the development.

This sequence was repeated over and over again. As a result, companies with disjointed systems, duplicated data, and redundant functionality are now the rule rather than the exception. Full integration of corporate data and functionality in a comprehensive architecture is now a target for many companies, but it's a target that will take several years and many dollars to hit.

Many enterprises that are now considering the integration of their systems and data have serious qualms about costs and chances for success. More than a few companies have been burned in the past when they attempted very large scale Data Processing projects. Executives who ask, "What will be different this time?" have every right to be concerned; particularly when there is no clear identification of the lessons learned from previous attempts.

Many executives have also recognized that companies that are making progress in integrating their data are using this integration to improve their business processes and are gaining some measure of strategic advantage. In several industries—banking, transportation, communications—companies are trying to play catch the leader by taking steps to establish long-term programs that integrate systems and data. This is generally good, except that it sometimes means that less attention is being paid to current systems and data. These are left to limp along as best they can until the cavalry (also known as the new systems environment) shows up. This state of affairs is not reassuring to the parts of the organization that need help with business problems today.

A strong case can be made for committing resources to developing an integrated data repository for the enterprise when there are also tangible returns in the short term.   Activities which help the enterprise make better use of the data it already has can provide valuable insights that can be applied to a long-term solution. At the same time, they can support process improvement in current operations.

Value is added to information through its use. If the toy producer's marketing department examines sales information and recognizes that industrial-grade plastic is replacing metal as the material of choice in toy truck purchases, new marketing initiatives can be developed to help sell the current inventory of metal trucks.

If the toy producer's manufacturing division sees the same data, it can adjust its long-term commitments to purchase metal and allocate some resources to examining the problems associated with a switch from metal fabrication to use of industrial plastics.

The distribution department can consider the impact on packing and shipping costs. The R&D group can begin searching for people with expertise in working with the plastics that will be used in future products.

The same data can be used in several different ways by different parts of the enterprise, each of which uses it to develop meaningful information. In most companies this sharing of data doesn't happen, and the reason it doesn't happen is testimony to the effects of project-based information planning.

The manufacturing, shipping, and R&D departments don't use the marketing data because they don't know it exists. The data they know about is the data that they specified for their own systems. In many companies, the only shared data is often the summary financial data associated with the annual budget process and the company's quarterly reports. There must be a way to do better than this.

Some enterprises are doing better. A medium-sized manufacturing concern in Pennsylvania developed an approach that has led to some success in turning departmental information into true corporate information without requiring a major overhaul of all the company's systems.

What the company did was to hire two computer science graduates who had previously worked for them through a university co-op program. Rather than putting their new employees to work in the Data Processing group, the company invested almost a year putting them through all of its internal training courses, and putting them to work with salesmen, manufacturing supervisors, distribution schedulers, personnel clerks, and financial planners.

At the end of this time, the two new employees were turned loose on the databases (or so-called databases) used by the company's systems. Their mission was to find all the data that might be useful to each department in the company and work out a way to get the data distributed where it would do the most good. They were to be the "Information Evangelists."

A number of interesting things started happening.

First, the actual use of personal computers increased significantly. Reports produced for one department are now routinely available as files that can be downloaded for data extraction by another department. The Data Processing department has moved some of its staff from mainframe programming jobs to jobs supporting the users' PCs.

Second, end-user programming began in earnest. Users who found that useful data was available to them from the corporate mainframe did not wait for DP support to access it. They developed PC-based procedures using commercial packages, usually databases or spreadsheets. There has been some concern about this within the DP group since end-user computing may mean a cutback in DP manpower, but there hasn't been any pressure yet from the users to make this happen.

Third, Data Processing management is now finding it easier to get inter-departmental backing for system development initiatives. Since it has been demonstrated that DP can play a key role in extending the information available to user departments, the credibility of the DP group has been raised within the company. This increased credibility combined with direct user experience in the value of wider data access has moved discussions of inter-departmental computing out of the buzzword category.

Fourth, the Information Evangelists have identified several large data-bases which simply weren't being used. The databases just sat out on the disks and received a few updates from some of the older programs. They were not used in preparing any reports and there were no inquiries being done against them. The data that they contained were either no longer of interest, or had been duplicated in other databases. The Information Evange-lists also found a complete manufacturing process database for a product line which had been dropped several years previously. The only "valuable" infor-mation it contained was the item numbers for the spare parts. The parts department occasionally checked the database if a part was ordered which didn't appear on the parts list available through their PC.

Fifth, a few business practices were streamlined as departments became more willing to use data captured by other parts of the enterprise. In a few instances multiple uncoordinated files containing the same basic data have been consolidated. Many of these files were on systems developed, designed, and used by individual departments within the company. The DP group has not been doing a hard sell on this issue, although it is a result which was hoped for.

In general, private databases are regarded as a means for control by departments who collect and maintain them. If the Data Processing group wants to integrate itself more effectively into the mainstream of the enter-prise, heavy-handed attempts to eliminate these private databases will be counterproductive. Convincing users, rather than attempting to coerce them, is the only way to wean them from their private stock of data.

While the Information Evangelist program has been very successful in helping the users understand the problems and possibilities of working with systems, it has had less of an effect within the Data Processing group. The exception to this is the effect on the Information Evangelists themselves.

Because of the nature of their work, the Information Evangelists have come to feel that they are in some sort of limbo. The users appreciate what they are doing. DP management appreciates the goodwill that they have won for the Data Processing organization. The database designers within Data

Processing find that the Information Evangelists are a great source of information.

However, the Information Evangelists are not very close to the programmers and analysts who make up the bulk of the Data Processing organization. Several programmers and analysts resent the corporate visibility that has been given to two junior members of the staff.

They resent the fact that the Information Evangelists have forged good working relationships with some of the users who had previously turned to members of the Data Processing staff for information or help with their systems. Some members of the DP staff worry that the expansion of end-user computing will limit their own opportunities to work on interesting projects. The emerging plans for consolidation of data and standardization of data access are causing anxiety because they reduce the value of specialized knowledge about the older systems.

Frankly, I'm lost in trying to figure out a solution for this problem. Perhaps the best approach is to make sure the individuals who were closely tied to users in the past learn enough about the new systems environment to continue their advocacy. I believe it is counterproductive to attempt to break down user/technical staff links unless they turn out to be abnormally disruptive.

Ideally, the goal should be to have every member of the Data Processing organization function as an Information Evangelist. In practice this may be difficult to achieve. Not everyone in the Data Processing staff will want to do this work. Some of the people may have problems in working with users. Some may not feel comfortable about leaving the shelter of their specific expertise.

One reason why the junior staff members were able to do an effective job as Information Evangelists was that they had no emotional investment in the company's existing systems. They weren't aware that "marketing doesn't get along well with engineering," so they persisted until they found people who were willing to see the advantages in getting information which came from other parts of the organization.

Another reason for their success was that they, as junior staff, were not regarded as an expensive or scarce resource. This meant that they were left alone during their training period and during the period when they started to spread the word about available data. There was no pressure to pull them away from what they were doing because they had none of the specialized knowledge needed to maintain the company's current systems.

It also helped greatly that the Data Processing manager kept them shielded from most of the day-to-day problems. The Information Evangelist program was the Data Processing Manager's idea, and she was determined to give it every opportunity to work.

So far, it seems to be working well.

Evangelists in the Warehouse

IBM's recent announcements include the concept of the "Information Warehouse." This is to be a store of information in many varieties from many sources, supporting flexible and powerful tools that allow users to inquire and retrieve data in a variety of ways. The executive who wishes to understand how well production scheduling was correlated with sales generated by the Mid-Atlantic sales campaign need only ask, and the requisite information will be provided.

It all sounds plausible. Technology exists which can store enormous amounts of information. Tools for information retrieval are becoming increasingly sophisticated. It's even possible to purchase specialized computers that are optimized for the efficient control of data storage devices.

Unfortunately, the problem of not knowing where to look for the desired data remains. We are still at the mercy of the indexers.

When faced with the need to extract a small amount of data from a large collection, it's a matter of faith that we will start by looking at some sort of index. The index may be the card catalog in a library, the table of contents for a user manual, an index of advertisers in a magazine, or any of a number of other forms. Indexes are provided to give a compact guide to the larger body of data which contains the sought-after details.

There is a terrible feeling of being cast adrift when an index doesn't contain anything with a recognizable connection to the data we are looking for. The frustration of having a large reference book with an inadequate index is enormous. It forces us to spend time we had not planned on and interrupts our train of thought.

As we move to ever larger collections of data, whether in centralized or distributed form, the importance of the indexing task will grow. With business data, the problem of doing the indexing job effectively is compounded by changes in data usage that can make yesterday's indexing scheme inappropriate for today's changed business environment.

To deal with the indexes that we have today, a class of software called "browsers" has been developed to assist users in locating and accessing data. The data may be program fragments, competitive business analyses, or any other type of data that can be stored and classified. Browsers are improving with the increased availability of technologies like Artificial Intelligence and

Neural Networks, but we do not yet have a way to identify the "best data" to support a query if there is more than one choice. That's because the definition of what is best is made by the user, who is outside the system.

Before the Information Warehouse concept was developed, IBM had proposed Information Centers which would be staffed by people who would work as reference librarians, guiding users to the data they needed. The idea is sound, but it requires that the staff have an in-depth knowledge of the environment that generates the queries. The Information Evangelist functions as a sort of reference librarian, with all the scope and flexibility implied by the comparison.

The level of investment required to develop the level of staff knowledge required to make the Information Center work effectively is substantial. The payoff from an effective Information Center is better use of corporate data. The payoff can be substantial, but it is difficult to quantify it a priori.

The most effective argument for setting up an Information Evangelist program may well come from measuring the cost of accumulating and storing data, and comparing that cost to the level at which the data is actually distributed and used as a normal business practice. If the effort and cost of collection can be shown in some way to exceed the level of usage, it may be possible to initiate the evangelist program as a means of getting "more bang for the bucks we've already invested."

Whatever the approach to getting started, the development of an information evangelist program is likely to provide a significant payback. You may even learn a few things about all that data you've been managing.

12

Software Development Statements Considered Harmful

Cognitive dissonance is alive and well in the software business. Proof of this can be found at any gathering focused on the problems of software engineering. Everyone present will acknowledge the fact that the vast majority of energy, money, and increases in functionality are found in the "support" or "maintenance" portion of the system life cycle. Following acknowledgment, this fact will be ignored.

The focus of software engineering remains firmly fixed on the development of new systems. Software engineering continues to be hypnotized by the vision that, "The next system will be perfect." Support for this point of view remains elusive. Today's imperfect systems are the perfect systems we tried to build only yesterday.

Proponents of software engineering need to accept the fact that the future that they talked about is now here, and it does not match the visions that they held for it. Instead of cries for new vigor in pursuing yesterday's visions, those who have a stake in the effectiveness of software engineering would do well to stop and see what the present situation offers. It is time to give more than lip service to the idea that we must learn to live with the billions of lines of code that already exist.

Systems of the future begin with the systems of today. It has been said, with justification, that "There is no software development. There is only radical maintenance."[1] The customers for tomorrow's systems will base their expectations on experiences with today's systems. Tomorrow's systems will be required to carry forward the data that was accumulated yesterday. The functionality of tomorrow's systems will be defined by reference to the functionality of today. The degree to which new software can truly be new is constrained by the systems that exist now.

Despite this, systems already in place are given scant notice in software engineering conferences, articles, and books. When existing systems are mentioned they are often treated as a problem that must be overcome. Study of the current system is circumvented in the process of developing requirements and specifications so that the new system will not "perpetuate the errors we have today." In a very real sense, software engineering makes no attempt to understand the past and, as a consequence, often repeats it.

By continuing to focus on the development of new software, software engineering has, ironically, delayed the introduction of engineering discipline to the task of software development. The practice of learning from mistakes and applying that knowledge to succeeding projects is a hallmark of all established branches of engineering. In software mistakes are buried, often before they're even cold.

Shortcomings in the current system are dealt with by the announcement that they will be corrected in the new system. The bugs in the current software will be fixed, but these will be treated as minor issues—even if there are enough of them to justify an interim release. However, detailed analysis of the nature of discovered defects and the underlying conditions that caused them is so rare as to be virtually nonexistent. If we take the reasonable position that widespread acceptance and use of software metrics is a sign that software engineering is finally living up to its name, where should we say the industry is today?

The Terrible Cost of Progress

The focus on a software development approach that demands that we continue to build new programs with new tools has denied us a history. Lacking a thread to connect the way we worked a few years ago with the way we work today, the degree to which our software is improving remains a matter

---

1. This comes from Charles Bachman, founder of Bachman Computer Systems.

of opinion. A conscious effort to disassociate new development activities from those of the past further impedes our ability to learn from prior experience. Current systems are often belittled unfairly in an attempt to justify the funding required for new software development.

As new tools and techniques are announced, they are presented as breaks with the past. I have lost count of the number of articles that tell me that I must discard my current ways of thinking about software as a first step in understanding object-oriented techniques or non-procedural languages.

Although a steady stream of new tools and techniques has come forth, their effect on software development practices has fallen well short of expectations. Even established tools, such as PC-based CASE, have achieved only a small fraction of the market penetration that was originally forecast for them. This is the natural consequence of an approach to tool and technique development that relies on revolution rather than evolution. Tools and techniques that demand a clean break from current practice simply have little to offer an enterprise that spends the majority of its computing effort and money on the modification of systems that already exist.

It is time for our industry to become more conscious of what we do and why we do it. A disproportionate amount of attention is being lavished upon software development, an activity that accounts for less than one quarter of the software functionality and cost of essential systems. Software engineering has become mesmerized by the work of designing tips for icebergs.

Real Problems Need Real Solutions

What is needed is a concentration on software refinement, not additional investment in software development methodologies. In several cases, development is no longer considered viable. Many of the critical systems used today in industry and government have grown so large and complex that the cost and disruption associated with their replacement by a new system can significantly affect overall corporate performance. One telecommunications company recently estimated the cost to replace a 17-year old system at $142 million. This estimate, large as it is, must also be evaluated in light of the fact that successful completion of very large software development projects on time and within budget is an uncommon occurrence. This is a daunting business proposition, and one can empathize with the management as they search for a satisfactory alternative.

The current state of software engineering offers little help. Its underlying premise is that the programs and systems currently in use must be replaced. Only then will the promised benefits materialize.

The re-usability of design and program elements promised by development-oriented software engineers is predicated on the idea that new elements will come into existence that can then be re-used. There is virtually no discussion of methods that could "recycle" existing code or put it in "recyclable" form.

Similarly, the problems associated with migration from current systems to new ones are passed over with the explanation that code will become "portable." Again, development of portable new code is assumed. Associated issues, such as the maintenance of data integrity during the migration process, receive virtually no attention.

A move from software development to software refinement implies considerably more than a minor adjustment to terminology. The development of a general approach to systems refinement is a complex intellectual challenge. The analysis and classification of general classes of constraints will require more than abstract reasoning; it will require empirical verification. One of the burdens of a general approach to systems refinement is that it must be applicable to systems as they are, not as we would like them to be.

It seems probable that systems refinement will be far more dependent upon automated tools than systems development is. A high degree of consistency in analyzing current software is critical in the refinement process. The individual programming styles represented in existing programs make evaluation by human readers difficult. "Automated assistants" that can identify logical structures and activity paths will almost certainly be required in order to effectively use a refinement methodology.

What Software Refinement Must Do

A refinement methodology needs to deal with at least three aspects of systems. The first aspect is defect identification and removal. Defects can be defined to embrace pathological linkages, unsynchronized changes to data, process and data redundancies, and other features that have the potential to cause errors or to increase the instability of the software as it is modified over time. The development of guidelines to be followed in this area is a formidable task.

The second aspect is that of modularity. The capability of the current system to support refinement must be enhanced by improving the independence of its component parts. It is reasonable to expect that some of the principles of structured design and object-oriented construction can be applied in this area.

The third aspect is that of restructuring. A key consideration is simplification—reducing the number of component parts in the system. This involves the difficult task of evaluating the quality of a design as opposed to verifying its legality under a given set of rules.

A refinement methodology should not be viewed as an adjunct to existing development methodologies. It is a replacement for the current system life cycle approaches which establish barriers between development and support activities.

The idea that the development cycle and the support cycle of a system are somehow separate must be discarded. Software engineering must begin to look at information systems as a progression of tools that link users and data. The data and its use represent an asset to the enterprise that must be nurtured and preserved. A refinement approach leads to increased asset value by improving the systems in an incremental manner. The development approach "rolls the dice" and predicts a big win.

The management of software activity must change along with the methodology. The common separation of development and support personnel acts as a barrier to a software refinement approach. There are far too many instances of systems being "thrown over the wall" from development to support. Rather than constructing an intricate series of procedures to transport software gently over the barrier separating development and support, ways must be found to tear the barrier down.

The discipline of software engineering, which has been focused on software replacement since its inception, faces the challenge of developing a general approach to software refinement. The cost to American enterprise of software engineering's "scorched earth" policy regarding existing systems has been immense. The gains have not been commensurate with the cost. What value can be put on the effort required to construct thousands of programs that determine the day of the week or sort a list of items?

We need to understand that these costs have been paid because books, articles, and seminars on software engineering have consistently endorsed the creation of new programs. The time has come to salvage what we can from the efforts of the past fifteen years and re-focus our energies on what we realistically expect the next fifteen years to bring.

In his well-known article, "No Silver Bullet,"[2] Frederick Brooks discusses the difficulty of developing information systems software. His description of the complexity, changeability, and external pressures for conformity that are typical of software systems points to the need to grow soft-

---

2. Frederick P. Brooks, Jr., "No Silver Bullet," *Computer*; April 1987.

ware over time rather than to build it as a single event. Software Engineering that consistently advocates replacement rather than refinement deals with the inherent problems of software by denying them. The search for the Silver Bullet is still going strong.

It's time for software engineering to put its fascination with the new in check and figure out how to get to next month rather than the next century.

Why is All This Important?

Software engineering provides models, assumptions and techniques for the software process that Data Processing managers manage. It has a significant influence on the tools that are developed for use as part of that process. The software process is one that managers have been struggling (sometimes successfully) to improve for over twenty-five years.

The study of software engineering has established a forum for the communication of ideas and experiences through a wide variety of organizations, publications, and conferences. It has discovered that interest in its subject is maintained by talking about what's new. The fragmented, low-status world of working with ten-year old COBOL programs does not easily allow development of standard approaches or exciting new methodologies.

The Data Processing manager who is trying to do the best she can, where she is, with what she already has will look for ways to make life easier for both herself and her staff. If all that software engineering has to offer is the "all or nothing" approach of restarting from scratch, the manager can be excused if she feels that current visions of long-term improvement in Data Processing are unrealistic. Software engineering will be regarded as irrelevant.

For such opinions to be widely held within the Data Processing community would be a disaster of the first order. The fact is that we have been able to improve the software process by observing it and measuring it. A substantial contribution to this improvement was the work done by people who established software engineering as a discipline. Improvements in software development have been realized from software engineering work in the areas of structured programming and analysis, and database design. However, software development is not the pressing problem it was when software engineering came into existence. For its own sake and for the sake of the Data Processing industry, software engineering needs to get back on track and look at the problems which need to be solved today.

13

Technical Management and Technical Competence

Technical competence is an individual attribute. We judge our own technical competence by our ability to make the computer do productive work. If we can develop programs that do what we said they would, and we do it without making a lot of obvious mistakes, we feel good about ourselves. We believe that our work reflects our competence. The sense of technical competence builds as we work on more complex projects and different tools. It's bolstered as we read books and magazines and become familiar with the products and services available in the market.

However, individual technical competence is seldom measured in any organized manner. Events such as Programmer's War Games (staged by the Atlantic Systems Guild) and similar technical competitions are so rare as to be almost nonexistent. The external evaluation of technical competence is largely subjective, much like the self-evaluation.

Consider the process you use when you hire technical staff for the systems organization. You ask your own technical people to interview the prospective employee. Each staff member asks questions from his or her own base of experience, trying to find out if the candidate has done things which are recognizable, or whether she is familiar with some of the terminology your people use. What emerges from this process is a subjective evaluation. Once the person joins the firm, you can be pleasantly surprised or unpleasantly disappointed by the way the new employee's actual performance matches your expectations.

This lack of an objective measure persists in the face of studies that show that technical competence varies greatly between individuals. Harlan Mills[1] claims that there is a 10 to 1 difference between the most and least productive programmers. Observers at the Programmer's War Games have reported even higher differentials in competitions where all of the participants were regarded by their employers as competent programmers. There is considerable debate about the effects of different languages and programming tools, as well as about the measures of productivity used. Nevertheless, it is indisputable that software practitioners have a significant range of ability.

While it is often possible to examine code or design prepared by two different people and make a judgement as to the relative competence of the two individuals involved, neither person's work is being compared to a standard. The standard doesn't exist. If it did, we would have tools like contractor's estimating books that provide norms for common tasks.

A *System Project Estimating Book* would allow us to calculate the time required to produce a functioning report, as well as the probable size of the program. We could use factors such as the type of database management system, number of fields in each report line, number of report sections, number of logical subtotals, number of sorts, and the programming language used as inputs to our calculations. Then, using the book, we could calculate an expected level of effort to complete the design, programming, testing and installation efforts.

Upon actual completion of the job, we would review the time, cost, and physical characteristics of the program; comparing them to the estimates created from information in the book. If the person doing the programming completed the job well under the estimate and the program's characteristics generally conformed to our calculations, we would conclude that her competence was above average. We would apply similar criteria to the person whose time to complete the job significantly exceeded the norms in the estimating book, or whose program differed widely from the expected characteristics.

---

1. Harlan Mills, *Software Productivity*, (Little, Brown, 1983.)

The *System Project Estimating Book* would also contain norms for other technical activities, such as designing and setting up local area networks, designing and building instrumentation interfaces, and preparing project budgets. There is more than enough empirical data in the Data Processing industry to support the development of this kind of book, but little of that data is organized or standardized. Once again, lack of timely, accurate data stands in the way of process improvement.

Very, very few enterprises have taken the time and effort to set up meaningful software metrics programs. The companies that have are gathering the data they need to create an estimating book that is particularly useful because it applies to their own systems development and maintenance environment. The Data Processing groups who have standardized on the Function Point Analysis method may find they have a powerful tool at their disposal. It helps eliminate some of the subjectivity associated with estimating and measurement.

In addition to supporting the estimating process, data that shows norms and performance ranges within the organization provides a point of reference for the individual who is trying to become more competent. It's certainly better than trying to measure one's self against a perception of the competence of one's fellow workers.

Reliable, documented competency norms across industry segments will not be available for a long time, if ever. It's not that there is some technical barrier in developing these norms, it's just that the effort to do so is small and fragmented. Individual researchers are attempting to track project data from several hundred firms, but this data attracts the interest of only a very few enterprises. Without a program to measure competency and productivity within the enterprise, data on how other enterprises are doing cannot be correlated. Developing a plan of action to improve individual technical skills will remain largely guesswork.

The issue of technical competence is compounded at the technical management level. The manager of a systems project needs to be concerned not only with the skills of the individuals, but also with the competence of the team as a unit. We still have very limited understanding of what makes one team effective and another hopelessly inept.

Although systems have been constructed by teams of analysts and programmers for many years, we cherish the idea that really good systems are the product of a single imagination.

This isn't true.

There's no denying the fact that original ideas are produced by individuals. But what happens to these ideas is that they are refined by groups—

small groups at first, larger ones later. Within these groups individual technical competence has the ability to advance or retard progress toward a cohesive vision of the system. In the final analysis, however, the system which comes forth is the product of many minds and many hands. We need to recognize the differences between the seed idea and the product which grows from it.

The management of many minds in the systems development or maintenance environment is a complex undertaking. A good analogy is that of a jazz quartet. One of the members of the quartet will establish a melody. The other members will contribute what they consider to be reasonable harmony and counterpoint, sometimes changing the melody as well. What emerges can be beautiful music, but the process is repeatable only in a general sense.

Nevertheless, the process is extremely important and it can serve as a lesson for technical managers. The jazz quartet process is capable of creating a wide variety of music. It is the consistent high quality of their music that distinguishes the best groups from the less successful. The jazz process is somewhat like the systems process in the way that both differ from manufacturing. Neither the jazz nor the systems process has the objective of producing multiple copies of a standardized output.

The fact that process outputs are always changing is a key reason for the difficulty in improving either jazz or systems performance. There are too many variables present to allow sustained concentration on just one of them. Systems may be even more difficult than jazz because there is no allowance for practice time.

The management of the jazz quartet yields a common effort that relies on individual contribution and competence. Technical managers try to foster the same atmosphere in the groups they manage. Technical management seems to work best when it provides a platform for the growth of individual technical competence. The best measurement of managerial competence is probably the degree to which individual competence grows. It is an indirect measure, and certainly imperfect, but it focuses on things which will be important to the enterprise over the long term.

The tools of the competent technical manager are a deeply-held belief in the importance of quality and a thirst to learn. These are hardly unique to the Data Processing business. Think of Frank Perdue and chickens, Henry Ford and automobiles, and Hyman Rickover and the nuclear navy. At its heart, management is an ethical undertaking. It communicates values as it communicates directives. The long-term prospects of the enterprise are dependent on the nature and communication of these values.

The practice of judging managerial competence on the basis of schedules met and budgets under-run emphasizes the transient values of the moment. It establishes no ties that join the employee to the enterprise. Worse, the "look at the short-term results" mentality is often applied against the technical staff to the exclusion of other measures. The often lamented propensity of Data Processing staff members to change employers on a frequent basis may have its roots in the "I don't care how you do it, just get the program working by Saturday," directives given by managers who are driven by schedule and budget only.

In point of fact, the questions of "Did you complete it on schedule? Were you within budget?" often reflect little more than laziness. Some managers play a perverted game by releasing incomplete and untested systems, and then pointing with pride to their budget and schedule records. In several companies, substantial executive bonuses are tied to budget and schedule performance, creating an environment where playing the game comes first, to the exclusion of the concern for the overall good of the enterprise. There are a few large and important enterprises that find that their ability to adapt and compete is slipping because narrow executive self-interest has been introduced into the systems process.

Managers who are concerned with the overall good of the enterprise, as well as the welfare of the people who work for them and their own mental well-being, need to focus on something other than budget and schedule. They need to focus on the thing that underlies improvements in productivity and which, in turn, makes possible long term improvements in the software process and in the value of the information asset. Managers who want these things need to be concerned with building a smarter company. They need to be concerned with what their technical staff is learning, and what they, themselves, are learning.

What should the technical manager want to learn? She should try to learn everything that has a bearing on quality. The manager should learn about the systems, tools, and methods being used, not only within her own enterprise, but also in other companies. She should learn what the individuals on her staff are really good at, what they think they're good at, and what they'd like to get better at. She should learn what her people are doing and help them to learn as they relate new lessons from work they are doing now to what they did before. Whenever she assigns one of the technical staff to a task, she should ask herself, "What is this person going to learn from this assignment?"

The technical manager should be cognizant of the fact that technical people learn a great deal from each other and should bed alert to opportunities that help to make this learning happen. She should take the lead in ensuring that periodicals and books with information that can be of benefit to the staff are available and freely circulated.

The technical manager should learn what the system users mean when they discuss the quality of the system, and what they mean when they talk about the quality of the work that the system supports. She needs to know how the users measure quality and then she needs to have the imagination to translate these measures into internal measures that can be understood by the technical staff.

There will be times when she needs to learn a technical subject in considerable depth and in a considerable hurry. Questions about the feasibility of using new technologies should never be left entirely in the hands of technicians. The technical manager needs to apply her perspective on the organizational, financial, and business process implications of the new technology. She needs a clear understanding of it in order to develop the proper questions.

Now, at the beginning of the 1990's, the technical manager needs to take the initiative to learn about new paradigms for Data Processing. Consider untestable systems. In many cases, such as global intelligent data communications networks, there is no rigorous way to test systems once they have been built. The size and complexity of the installed system cannot be economically duplicated in a test environment. Significant (several orders of magnitude?) improvement in preventing defects must be realized. As a practical matter, this means that the work at higher levels of abstraction must be flawlessly translated to the lower levels. It also means that the quality of work at the higher levels of abstraction must be massively improved. These are not just technical problems, they are management problems, and they must be solved.

The keys to successful technical management are the thirst to learn, the capacity to do it, and the ability to communicate what has been learned. Technical managers don't need to have a body of relevant technical knowledge as a pre-condition of assuming a technical management role, but they need to understand what they don't know. The manager's recognition of her need to educate herself about the technology and the way she goes learning what she needs to know can be a very positive element in building an effective team when it happens in public and establishes a tone.

Good managers are always trying to learn something new, and they are concerned with ensuring that those they work with are also engaged in the learning process. Intellectual curiosity can be found wherever outstanding technical leadership is found, and this is not a coincidence. Individual technical competence seems to cluster around competent technical managers as well. This is also no coincidence.

Competence, Management, and Asset Value

Technical competence and management effectiveness are critical in getting the most value from the information asset. The value of the asset is derived from the use of the data. The technical competence and management skills of the Data Processing group provide the mechanics for delivering the data to its users.

The ability to respond quickly and effectively to the changing needs of these users depends upon both the skills and direction of the Data Processing staff. Data Processing managers can stifle the ability of their groups to support the enterprise if they neither understand nor support the use of tools or techniques that can significantly improve productivity and quality.

The work of the Data Processing staff is becoming increasingly sophisticated as systems are made to work in concert, and as the use of computers expands to additional areas of activity. The problems that programmers and analysts are wrestling with today are not the same as those faced fifteen years ago. Nevertheless, many Data Processing staffs are seeing little change in the tools or environment they use. Many systems, perhaps the majority, are still being programmed line-by-line in COBOL, "C," or other established procedural languages. Programmers and analysts are still forced to subdivide problems into ever smaller steps to determine the programming logic that is appropriate to the task at hand. Computer Aided Software Engineering (CASE) software still languishes; its initial promise of broad productivity increases remains unfulfilled.

The technology infrastructure of an enterprise is more than the power of its central computers or the number of workstations and LANs. It includes the abilities of the Data Processing staff. An approach to funding based on the long-term commitment of a percentage of the information asset value allows for investment in staff and management skills on a continuing basis, not on the basis of pilot project approval.

Today, development of technical competence and management skills in most enterprises proceeds almost as a form of guerilla warfare. A new tool or technique is discovered by a member of the technical staff. The staff member then tries to convince other staff members that the group should "try this one out." A likely piece of work is identified and the new tool or technique is bundled with this already-requested job as a pilot proposal. Sometimes the proposal is accepted, sometimes it isn't. In virtually every case, the learning curve associated with new ways of doing things is underestimated because it is necessary to minimize the cost of the proposal in order to gain approval.

When the pilot project is completed, there is seldom, if ever, a cohesive plan to objectively evaluate the effects of the new approach. There is rarely a mechanism for disseminating what has been learned to other members of the Data Processing staff. There is rarely a concerted effort to understand the changes in management skills required by new technologies or techniques. In many cases the task of collecting accurate data to measure the performance of the pilot project is left undone.

A more constructive approach to experimentation with new technical approaches is to first identify those members of the Data Processing staff who are regarded by their peers as technical leaders, and make them the focus of an appropriately funded effort to improve staff effectiveness. "Appropriately funded" is not meant to signify carte blanche for the purchase of every "breakthrough of the week" which comes along. It is meant to signify a level of funding which allows technical leaders to subscribe to a wide range of publications, become members of relevant organizations and attend conferences where they can get information that goes beyond the material in glossy marketing brochures. It is also meant to signify a level of funding that will be committed to purchase hardware, software or training if there is good evidence that these are appropriate to the working practices of the Data Processing organization and the needs of the enterprise. Further, it is meant to be a funding basis that will tolerate mistakes as long as something useful is learned from them.

Just as a company needs information evangelists to promote more extensive use of the data managed by the Data Processing organization, it also needs technology evangelists to encourage the Data Processing staff to develop new skills. The impetus to develop these skills must come from within the staff, or it is likely to fail. Executive dictums that "we will use CASE" or "we will adopt a 4GL" have achieved virtually identical results over the years. They haven't succeeded.

The use of an asset based funding approach provides more than just funding for skills development. It also provides a compelling reason to invest time in improving technical competence and in improving the effectiveness of management practices. Improved effectiveness goes straight to the bottom line in reducing costs and delivering more value to the user. This, in turn, ensures additional funding for further improvement.

I do not know how to properly quantify the asset value of technical and management competence in a Data Processing organization. A fair measure might be that of competitive advantage based on the ability to bring products or services to market more quickly than one's competitors. The idea of establishing productivity benchmark values and quantifying subsequent improvements mirrors the approach to quantifying asset value for the data, but this is far more subjective since the nature of Data Processing work is changing rapidly.

It may be possible to establish a quantitative asset value for Data Processing skills by using some form of software process model, such as the process maturity models based on the work of Watts Humphrey[2] or the more detailed software process models that are becoming available[3]. If this happens, it will be a considerable benefit to Data Processing managers and staff, many of whom have become frustrated by the knowledge that they could improve their performance if they were given the time and resources necessary to do so.

---

2. Watts Humphrey, *Managing the Software Process*, (Addison-Wesley, 1989.)

3. *Software Project Dynamics* by Tarek Abdel-Hamid and Stuart Madnick, Prentice Hall, Englewood Cliffs, NJ, 1991, is a book which should be on your bookshelf if you are concerned with improving the software process.

14

Starting
Smaller

In Data Processing, it seems as though everything that we're asked to do is big. Are we thinking of developing an enterprise model? That's a big job. How about introducing a new methodology? That's a big change in the way we work. Suppose we decide to re-engineer some of our older systems? That could mean a big impact on our staff.

Part of the reason that Data Processing in many enterprises is stuck in a rut of piecemeal projects is that there is a reluctance by those who control the funding to undertake big efforts when the reward cannot be clearly seen.[1] A question like: "How much money is rewriting the order entry system using this object-oriented stuff going to save me next year?" is neither ignorant nor facetious. It's a legitimate business question that deserves a better answer than it usually gets. Big projects don't get off the ground without the answers to some big questions

---

1. An interesting view of this situation comes from a retired AT&T systems executive who claimed that there are only two types of projects—the ones that are too small to deserve executive attention and the ones that are too big and complex to undertake.

first. Even more modest projects need to answer these hard questions in times when money is tight.

It is a reasonable idea that one should determine the asset value of all the data and systems used by the enterprise. Many of us can see ways in which this information could be used to bring additional rationality into the funding and project prioritization process. The temptation may be great to immediately propose an effort to collect and organize the needed details. This suggestion is unlikely to meet any real resistance until the scope and cost of the effort are laid out.   All of a sudden, it will be recognized as a big project.   At that point the work of gathering system and data details will be identified by those who foot the bill as yet another grandiose scheme thought up by Data Processing.

For those of us who would like to initiate some changes in the way Data Processing does business without having to fight the battle of getting a big project approved, there needs to be a way to start small.

Situation Assessments

Collecting a full set of value information *is* a big job. It takes time and effort to do it all and to do it right. Nevertheless, it's possible to make significant inroads into the job without waving a red flag in front of those who don't like large projects. One of the most effective ways of getting started is to introduce the practice of situation assessments. "Situation Assessment" is the two-dollar phrase for looking before you leap.

The goal of the situation assessment is to determine the best way to handle a proposed change to the existing systems environment. For any proposed change there are a number of possible solutions:

- •Build a new system that includes all the functionality of the current system plus the new functionality that's needed.

- •Build a new sub-system to handle the new functionality and link it in some way to the current system.

- •Add programs and/or files to the current system to provide the new functionality.

- •Re-engineer all or part of the current system to support both current and new functionality.

- •Purchase or otherwise obtain a system that provides the new functionality, and merge it into the current environment.

- Purchase or otherwise obtain a system that provides both the current and new functionality, and migrate data and operational practices to use it.

- If the issue is primarily one of capacity, establish a copy of the current system and provide some form of data partitioning between the current system and the copy.

- If the issue is primarily one of capacity, upgrade the hardware platform, or migrate to another platform with sufficient power to do the job.

- Reorganize both the business practice and systems environment to support a new, integrated practice that provides better quality and/or productivity than that which would result from simply adding new functionality.

- Merge all requests for new functionality and develop a general solution that goes beyond any single request.

- Develop an operational work-around.

- Don't do anything.

Establishing which of these approaches is the best, or even those that are relatively better than others, requires knowledge of available technology, knowledge of the business practices, (and impacts of the new functionality upon them) and knowledge of the benefits to the enterprise related to the new functionality. It also requires knowledge of the costs associated with the various approaches, and of the impacts of the proposed approaches on the existing environment of Data Processing. It is unlikely that all of this knowledge exists in a form that is readily available for use in an objective analysis.

What is needed is a situation assessment. After all, where you wind up will depend in no small way on where you start from. It's important to really understand where you are now before you attempt to do something new.

Situation assessments are a two or three person job, but you need the right people. You need a systems person who has some exposure to the current system or systems used in similar business situations. You need a user person who understands the business practices that need to be supported. The extra person might be a systems or user person who is not closely associated with the system or practices under consideration, but who is capable of asking the simple questions that often get overlooked by those too close to the subject matter. It often pays to use an outside consultant in this role, provided you get the right consultant.

As a practical matter I have found that it is fairly easy to set up teams like this for a short period—two to three weeks is about average. The work

can be done on a half-day rather than full-time basis, but the half-days need
to be scheduled and adhered to. The whole process of situation assessment is
an exercise in creative thinking and continuity of the effort is important to
keep the thought process going smoothly.

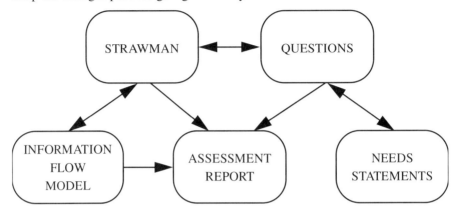

Figure 14-1 The Situation Assessment Process

Performing the Assessment

The first thing to do is to build a "strawman." The strawman is a description
of the desired business process. It provides the level of detail necessary to
identify the information needed to make the process work and the outcomes
of the practices which use the information. It is a picture of the business process the way it is intended to be.

It's important to understand what the strawman is *not*. It is not a
requirements document, although it may form the basis for one. The strawman is generally too informal to be used as a requirements statement for systems development. It is designed to be understood by those who have some
degree of familiarity with the business process being addressed.

The strawman is used to develop two more parts of the assessment. The
first is a list of questions which will be used to determine how well the current practices satisfy the business requirement described in the strawman. In
practice I have found that the job of developing the question list often leads
to further changes in the strawman as issues uncovered in the task of question creation stimulate thinking about what the process really needs to be.

In addition to questions about the practices, questions about the current
systems and the ways in which they support the practices also need to be
developed. These, too, can stimulate thinking about what the nature of the
process described by the strawman should be.

The second thing developed from the strawman is an information flow model of the process which the strawman describes. In point of fact, drawings are very often a part of the strawman and these drawings make a good jumping-off point to develop the information flow model. The information flow model is a more formal graphic representation of the business process, and it's a valuable tool when the current systems environment is examined.

The information flow model can easily be created using almost any modern CASE tool. Remember, this is a high-level model and it does not need to reflect the systems and data organization of the current Data Processing environment.

As information flow models are developed for multiple situation assessments, they can be brought together to form a fledgling Enterprise Model. The job of collecting and amalgamating the information flow models should be assigned to the Director of Data Processing or to one of her immediate staff. The Enterprise Model is too valuable a tool to be relegated to someone who is further down in the organization.

The job of developing the strawman, the questions and the information flow model typically takes four or five days when applied to the extension of a current business process. The job will take longer if the issue involves consolidation of existing business processes or the introduction of a completely new process.

The next step is to ask the questions. In asking questions about the current systems and practices, the information flow model serves as a point of reference for both those who are responsible for the situation assessment, and those who are attempting to answer the questions. The number of people who need to contribute to the question and answer process is typically fairly small. If the assessment is being done for an order-entry process, the people involved might include:

- An order-entry supervisor or experienced customer service representative
- A salesman who has regular contact with customers who place orders
- The person who is responsible for the initiative to make changes to the order entry process
- The systems analyst who has lead responsibility for the order entry system
- The person who has organizational responsibility for order entry

When we first started doing situation assessments, we interviewed a much larger group of people. The job took much longer, and we learned that longer didn't necessarily equate to higher confidence in the results. On several assessments, we encountered pressure to "run this by" people and organizations who were only marginally affected by the proposed changes. Company politics caused the pressure. In some of these assessments, we added extra questions and sent a questionnaire to the political contacts, requesting their input. These people seldom responded, but we could dutifully report that everyone was "in the loop."

The responses to the questions can lead to some additional changes in the strawman, and they can lead to additional questions as well. You need to keep in mind that situation assessment is only a high-level effort to select the most promising approach to solving the problem. It is not the problem's solution.   Typically, the question and discussion sessions take about two hours for each of the people interviewed, and the interviews can be completed in three days if there are no scheduling difficulties.

What comes out of the questions is a set of needs statements which capture the ways in which the current environment must change. Some typical needs statements are:

- There needs to be a mechanism for checking the customer's credit worthiness before the order is accepted.

- There needs to be a mechanism for providing different levels of assistance to customer service representatives who take orders on-line.

- There needs to be a confirmation mechanism for customers who send in their orders by fax.

- The order entry system needs to be available at least 98% of the time, and there needs to be a method of capturing order information when it is not available.

Needs statements are directed to the business process, the current system, the company organization, and any other aspect which needs to be addressed in achieving the changes presented in the strawman. However, the needs statements shouldn't constitute a "wish list" for all the things that users and programmers want to do.

The final task is for the assessment team to write a report with a recommendation. The report should include all of the supporting detail: the strawman, the questions, the answers, the information flow model, and the needs statements. It should identify the most critical issues affecting the choice of an approach, and it should recommend the approach to be taken to change the business process and its associated systems environment.

The Assessment Environment

Clearly, there is the potential for abuse. The situation assessment process can be used to "prove" the approach of forming a new corporate division with entirely new systems.[2]   Opposing this is the general understanding (that can be made an explicit directive) that the situation assessment process is designed to determine the most effective approach to the problem at hand in terms of achieving necessary business process objectives while minimizing cost, complexity and disruption to the business.

The good news is that situation assessments can provide substantial savings by killing ideas which were not well thought out before they turn into full-fledged projects.[3]   This is because assessments start by trying to get a real understanding of what the business process needs to be. This, in turn, points the way to identifying the problems that really need to be solved. Table 14-1 shows a few samples of situation assessment outcomes for assessments performed following the pattern that has been described here.

About twenty to twenty-five percent of the situation assessments I've been involved with have not been completed. The problem most often has been a political one. Either someone in authority decides that he doesn't want a study, (he wants something done and done now) or the discussions of the situation assessment are regarded as politically unpalatable.

Be that as it may, the practice of developing a standard approach to situation assessment reaches well beyond the problem at hand. Materials are produced that describe the business processes which are needed, the information flows that need to be present, and the relationship of the flows and processes to the current systems environment. This is the raw material that is needed to understand the importance of Data Processing to the enterprise by showing its role in the improvement of business processes. It's the stuff that goes into Enterprise Models. It is the information needed to bring some rationality to the overall systems planning process.

---

2. Gerald Weinberg has pointed out that feasibility studies rarely produce the answer, "This isn't feasible." I suspect that they reach that answer more often than they communicate it.
3. It's easier to produce a "Don't do this" recommendation from a small, informal group than from a large, high-visibility study team. With the small group, there aren't as many egos on public display.

Table 14-1 Situation assessment outcomes.

Business Process	Assessment Effort	Initial Approach	Recommended Approach
Order Entry	5 Person Weeks	Purchase New Commercial System	Improved Operator Training
Large Inventory Reporting	9 Person Weeks	Total Re-Write	Transmit Data to PCs for Report Development
Operator Scheduling	4 Person Weeks	Partition into Sub-Systems	Re-Write with 25% Re-Use of Current System Design and Code
Uncollected Receivables Tracking	5 Person Weeks	Purchase New Commercial System	Change to Relational Database & Consolidate Organizational Groups
Project Management	6 Person Weeks	Standardize on PC-based tool	Standardize on PC-based tool

The adoption of a standard approach to situation assessment is the sort of small start that sets in motion a process which gathers momentum over time. Virtually every enterprise does some form of situation assessment before it starts work on new or enhanced systems, but very few take the effort to standardize the process. As a result valuable information is gathered and then lost again.

There is a lot of concentration today on the re-use of code and systems design elements. Such re-use is touted as the key to major economic benefits through reduced cost and improved quality in systems development. If this is true for building pieces of code, we ought to consider the benefits that can accrue from re-using information about the business processes that the system supports. As a Data Processing manager, you ought to regard this type of information as one of *your* most valuable assets, one that you can use to generate benefits for the enterprise as a whole.

Real economic benefits come from building the right systems to do what the enterprise needs.

15

The Triumph of Clerical Computing

When computers were first introduced to commercial enterprises, there were no crowds of programmers and analysts waiting to receive them. What happened was that bright people from accounting, manufacturing, or whatever department would be using the computer were sent to schools run by the computer manufacturer to learn how to write programs. Once they had finished their training courses, these people proceeded to write programs that helped them solve problems directly related to day-to-day activity. The results of this approach were generally very good.

There was not a great deal of attention paid to analysis. The people who were writing the programs already understood the practices that were being automated. The practices that were selected were usually those that involved repetitive drudgery—exactly the sort of work that showed the computers to their best advantage. The success of these first attempts at automating business processes not only established the value of computers as business machines, but also led to career advancements for many of the people who programmed them.

As promotions came to the original programmers, the programs were handed over to others who, in many cases, did not fully understand the process that had been automated. The new programmers had not been exposed to conditions prior to the development of the systems they were being asked to maintain and expand. Frequently, the new programmers had been educated as data processing specialists and did not have a background in accounting, manufacturing, or the other user disciplines.

The users were changing, too. Many of the people whose jobs included some degree of interaction with the computer system had not been involved in defining the system's functionality. In many cases the new users requested new functionality that reflected their view of the job to be done. This was understandable. The shifting of mundane, repetitive functions to the computer had changed the way in which many jobs were performed.

It is interesting, and in some sense ironic, to note that the acceptance of mainframe clerical computing has parallels in the acceptance of personal computing. People who are intimately familiar with the business processes have learned to use personal computers to perform the repetitive and time-consuming work involved with creating budgets, preparing correspondence, and developing presentations. As the tools and techniques available for personal computing have become more involved, some of the PC work is being transferred to supporting staff members who are more familiar with the computer than they are with the business processes that the PC supports.

In most companies, the impression of what computers could and should do was based on what the computers were already doing. To many company executives, it seemed that what computers were already doing was producing massive piles of paper. Most programmers saw nothing inherently wrong with this state of affairs. Since computers could handle large volumes of data quickly, it seemed like a good thing to be able to provide summary and detailed data at the same time. Everything the user might want to know was in the reports. There was no need to disrupt operations with requests for special runs.

The information coming out of the computer began going to junior staff people who flipped through the pages, extracted the specific data their managers wanted, and put it in memos which were then placed on the managers' desks. Computers came to occupy a position where both their input and their output was supplied by clerks. The clerks might be called by any number of names, including Customer Service Representative and Assistant Purchasing Officer. Whatever the title, the job was to put data into the computer or take it out.

Corporate executives knew that the computers were there, but, for the most part, the executives were as isolated from the computers as they were from the clerical workers the computers replaced. Actually they were more isolated. Prior to the installation of computers, a billing clerk went through a number of human actions to generate the bill. If bills were being prepared incorrectly, the executive could directly influence the person who was causing the problems.

When there was a computer problem company executives were stymied. It was often unclear why the problem was occurring or what had to be done to correct it. The executives could not communicate in the language of Data Processing and came away frustrated when they attempted to do so. Even those who were associated with the original introduction of computers in the company were unable to understand how the computing work was now being done. Many companies had to call in consultants to assist management in understanding what was happening to the company's clerical data. This was almost unheard of when clerical work was still a manual process. In many companies, management came to believe that the Data Processing group and the expenses associated with it were both out of touch with reality.

Ironically, the Data Processing staff had come to inherit the same sentiments as the clerical workers that the computers replaced. The Data Processing staff felt that they were not appreciated by company management. The staff came to believe that management did not understood the work Data Processing had to do, did not realize that change and development requests were sometimes unrealistic, and clearly did not realize how important the Data Processing staff was to the business. In many cases there was some validity to these complaints.

The root of these misunderstandings is the fact that despite the success in automating functions critical to the health of the enterprise, clerical computing receives little respect in most companies. Even within the computer business, involvement with clerical computing is treated as a form of second-class citizenship. Describing someone as a "COBOL report writer" is not a way of bestowing praise in the Data Processing profession.

Clerical computing deserves genuine respect; not only in the enterprises where it plays a critical role in day-to-day operations, but also in the computer industry as a whole. Had clerical computing not been so successful, the computer business would not have the economic resources available to develop the wide variety of technology and software we take for granted today.

The value of clerical computing in business is staggering. One of the key reasons it receives as little respect as it does is that very few companies have taken the time to actually measure the benefits. Medium and large companies have reached the point where it is not feasible to consider large-scale clerical activity without Data Processing systems. New services have arisen because the computer supports the clerical work much more efficiently than manual procedures ever could. Would MasterCard™ and Visa™ have been possible without clerical computing?

Respected or not, the value of clerical computing will increase by an order of magnitude over the next decade. There are forces at work that will change the role of clerical computing in the enterprise. The changes will not be easy, but it's important to the health of the business enterprise that they take place. Clerical computing will serve as the foundation for the development of managerial and executive computing as widely accepted elements in normal business activity.

The first of the forces that will lead to change is the introduction and widespread acceptance of personal computers as managerial tools. People with management responsibility in service, sales, manufacturing, and other areas have learned to use PC spreadsheet programs to help deal with quantitative aspects of their jobs. In many cases the data entered into PC spreadsheets and databases is copied from printouts produced by the computers in the company's Data Processing department.

The personal computers do not represent a challenge to the clerical computing activities of the formal Data Processing organizations. I am not aware of any call to unplug the mainframe that has arisen because middle level managers learned to write macros for Lotus 1-2-3. Arguments that networks of personal computers can perform the functions of mainframes seem to collapse when confronted by the magnitude of clerical processing. What the personal computers have done is to provide automation at the point where clerical data is transformed into management information. They have enhanced the manager's ability to select, manipulate, and present information that is then used to affect organizational performance and strategy.

Many PC users have come to recognize clerical computing as the primary source of data for managerial computing. The role of the PC has changed from that of a stand-alone unit to one that is tied to other PC's and the mainframes. More and more clerical reports are now defined as files for transmission to PC's as opposed to hard-copy printing.

For managers, the advantages of these changes are three-fold. First, the information can be more current. Second, there is greater flexibility in organizing data to meet changing information requirements. Third, the presentation of the data can be easily adjusted to the format that the manager finds most effective. The increasing interest in "Executive Information Systems" and "Graphic User Interfaces" has been fueled by the improved access to information that can be provided by the personal computer or workstation.

A second force for change is the growing awareness by managers of the importance of quantitative information in accomplishing corporate goals. In this respect Data Processing is beginning to follow the path taken by financial management. The emergence of financial management as a key participant in corporate planning and policy is a recent phenomenon. It has been driven by the recognition of gains to be made by proactively using quantitative financial data.

The use of quantitative data for quality and productivity improvement is becoming recognized as an essential skill that must be mastered to compete effectively in global markets. Advances in technology allow data to be accessed and presented with greater flexibility at lower cost than has been previously possible. The need for better quantitative information is focusing management attention on the data that can be extracted from the clerical computing processes.

It is important that increased data use by managers be built on a solid foundation of clerical computing. The recognition of clerical computing's role in creating the information asset is going to fundamentally change the work performed by Data Processing personnel, especially as the importance of managerial and executive computing grows. The most noticeable aspect of this change will be the increased importance of business oriented analytical skills and associated communications skills when compared with the importance of technology oriented skills.

Data Processing for managerial and executive support is not merely an extension of clerical Data Processing. One might think of the difference between driving a cab in New York City and driving a racing car at the Indianapolis 500.   Current skills must be re-evaluated and new skills must be learned.

Achieving proficiency in business oriented skills is a much more complex task than learning to write programs and analyze data structures. It's not clear that the academic Data Processing curriculum in our universities will be able to adapt to the new requirements. The difficulty of developing good business/computer analysts will slow down the rate at which companies can take advantage of current and future technology.

The degree to which today's Data Processing staff can support changes in information usage in the enterprise will depend upon the vitality of their current environment. In many staffs where the primary focus is on fixing problems in existing systems, motivation to learn the business skills that compliment new technological developments is lacking. As rapid prototyping, visual programming, and non-procedural languages raise the level of abstraction at which Data Processing work is done, the detailed technical knowledge required to develop, modify, and operate systems today will become less valuable. This will be a wrenching experience for many Data Processing professionals whose career advancement has been built upon mastery of technical skills that are rapidly being devalued.

The increased sophistication of tools and systems that can manipulate clerical data will cause a further decline in the visibility of the clerical computing process. Industry has already made great strides in moving from the entry of data as a specialized function to the capture of data as part of normal business activity. Advances in voice and handwriting recognition will accelerate this trend. The creation of the clerical data will become more invisible.

Despite this, the strategic importance of clerical computing will continue to grow. The clerical computing processes themselves will be re-evaluated from the standpoint of capturing data that can be used as effective input to the management and executive processes. The wide variety of data capture and retrieval requirements will contribute to the growth of systems where the prime concern is data organization and administration throughout a network computing resource.

Figure 15-1 reflects the general characteristics of the classes of data which can be found in all enterprises. It is important to realize that the boundaries between the classes are not exact and that there is no formal means of delineating the ways in which data moves between the classes. Nevertheless, it is reasonable to believe that a product manager will want to know how many customers purchased her product during the last month and what the demographic characteristics of these customers was. She will also be influenced by what is written about her product in trade magazines. From all this, she may make the decision whether to increase the advertising budget, change the ads, or send the product back for further development. By analyzing the various kinds of data and correlating this information with what she already knows, her knowledge about the product and the market will increase.

It is knowledge, the organized and applicable information created from clerical, management, and external data, that provides an enterprise with a long-term competitive advantage. The key role of clerical data as an instrument in building knowledge needs to be recognized and acknowledged.

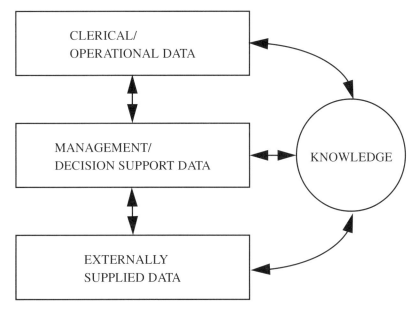

Figure 15-1 The Relationship of Data Classes

The challenge facing enterprises today is to build on the benefits that clerical computing has delivered. Just as the triumph of clerical computing was brought about by people who first saw the potential of computers in commercial business, extending the triumph from the clerical to managerial and executive functions of the enterprise will depend upon people who have a knowledge of the problems to be solved and the vision to see how technology might solve them.

Theirs will not be an easy task.

Conway's Law

It is sad but true that in today's Data Processing World, the majority of clerical systems can be cited as examples of Conway's Law: "Systems tend to resemble the organizations that built them." This situation makes it very difficult to replace or re-engineer these critical systems, even at the point when such action is clearly indicated.

To start at the beginning, it's necessary to state the obvious—programmers and analysts build the systems that they are allowed to build. That is to say, the projects that are funded are the ones that get worked on.

The people who provide the funds are almost always process-oriented. These system sponsors have responsibility for business processes such as accounting, shipping, personnel, and so forth. They want data processing systems that help their business processes. Many of these systems fall into the class of clerical systems.

In most enterprises, business processes and the systems that support them have owners. In a telephone company the Treasurer's department may own the remittance process that collects the payments and applies them to the accounts receivable. As the remittance process owner, the Treasurer's department will also sponsor funding for software that supports the remittance process. This is, for the most part, clerical software.

Because the invoicing process generates information that makes up a large part of the overall accounts receivable, some of the software development to support the remittance process will be in the form of changes to the invoicing system (a clerical system). The invoicing system is often owned by the telephone company's Billing department. As more changes are made to accommodate remittance as well as invoicing, the invoicing system takes on a structure and functionality that obviously serves different departments in different ways. This is exactly what Conway observed.

The situation Conway noticed came about even though individual systems projects were well managed and achieved their goals. The end result, however, is a systems environment that is very difficult to change and, at the same time, even more difficult to replace.

Conway's Law will continue to be relevant as long as projects focus on their contribution to individual business processes as a basis for funding. In this environment, functionality is added, not as part of an overall master plan, but in a piecemeal manner as funding is made available. Concerns about architectural integrity of clerical systems are often subordinated to pressing requirements for improvements in specific business processes.

Project managers in this situation are often helpless to do anything that preserves the architectural integrity of the system and its data.   They find that the scope and funding for the projects they work on are constrained by what the business process owner is willing to pay for. Attempts to go outside the constraints to address architectural issues are likely to be regarded by the project's business sponsor as unnecessary expenditures of time and money.

It is difficult to convince process owners that they have an interest in system issues beyond those that directly affect them. Most managers are faced with evaluations that stress cost containment and profit contribution. Getting funding for projects that do not have clearly defined payoffs in a clearly defined time is an uphill battle. There are very few tools available to help the manager who wants to spend time and money in order to understand the long-term consequences of a short-term project.

Improvement in the way that enterprise models are developed and presented holds the best chance of changing the current pattern. These models are the best available tool for showing the degree and importance of data sharing and system interaction.   Without the ability to communicate these things, the value of clerical systems and their sensitivity to change cannot be explained to the business process owners.

Unfortunately, many of the enterprise models built to date are seen as internal tools for the Data Processing organization. They do not include the business processes in a way that can be easily recognized by the process owners. This limits communications about what systems should and can do, and leaves us building a new generation of clerical systems that will eventually offer further proof of Conway's Law.

The sad fact of the matter is that Conway's Law leads to some terrible systems problems that don't have technical solutions. These problems don't even have a management solution within the Data Processing group itself. They are a consequence of the way that the enterprise is managed.

Data Processing, as a whole, is getting better about quality, estimation and other issues related to project management. However, it will be necessary to make fundamental changes in the ways that the enterprise manages its information asset. Companies must break the management patterns that constrain the effects of even the best Data Processing performance. Until this happens, the clerical systems which provide the foundation upon which the Data Processing of today is built will be competing with Conway's Law in a race they cannot win.

16

The Limits of Reusability

Reusability has emerged as an important topic over the past few years, and rightly so. Considerable cost reductions in software development are possible if you can avoid writing new code. By building new systems using system components whose high quality is already a matter of record, these savings can be extended over the entire life cycle.

However, reusability is not new and so far it hasn't had a major impact on the practice of software development. The projected dominance of the Ada programming language was based on the expectation that extensive libraries of reusable program modules would be available. The Japanese SIGMA project had much the same orientation. While part of the gap between expectation and results for these efforts can be attributed to inertia in the software industry, another element that contributes to the gap has become evident in hindsight. This element will be a continuing constraint on our ability to reuse the code and designs which we develop.

At some point, design and code must incorporate the context in which they are used. Without incorporating it, the ability of a system to support user practices is severely limited. Context may be as simple as specifying the order in which fields should appear on a report. It can be as complex as the integrated series of measurements and calculations needed to establish an output value in a process control environment.

In biology it is often noted that the degree to which an organism has evolved in adapting to a specific environment will limit the organism's ability to survive if the environment changes. The same is true for software.

In order to understand the relationship between software and its environment, it's necessary to recognize that software systems exist in two environments simultaneously. The first of these is the operational environment, where a system must be adapted to the features of the hardware and system software in order to run at all. The second is the environment where the benefits of the system will be realized by applying its functionality in support of normal business activity.

Reusability is harder to obtain in the elements that support business-related functionality. For example, the computations that show the danger of equipment failure based upon the readings from vibration detectors will be useful in the system that monitors equipment condition. No matter how neatly encapsulated, these computations are unlikely to be reusable in another context.

As with biological organisms, the system elements that have been developed to most effectively correspond to the context of their business environment will not be readily transferable to a different environment. For these elements, reusability is only possible when replacing a system with another system which embodies existing functionality. Even this may not be possible if the new operating environment differs significantly from the old.

The degree to which context incorporation is a problem is influenced by the system developers' desire to make the system useful to its end users. This means that external factors, such as the organizational structure of the business, can and do influence system design. More and more, there is a demand from operational departments that the introduction of new systems must be done in a way which minimizes operational disruption. As a consequence of these demands, the context of system usage becomes reflected in both the design and eventual implementation of the system. Long-term reusability considerations are sacrificed to the current (and very real) demands of the business.

Reusability today is generally oriented toward the operating environment. Even in Data Processing organizations that are otherwise inefficient, one can find the use of COPYLIBs or program skeletons incorporating standard error handling procedures. Reusability at this level is not to be sneezed at. If estimates made by some leading edge software developers are correct, seventy-five percent of future program code will be concerned with managing the user interface. This, in turn, means that the savings related to reusability of system elements that manage the operating environment will be significant.

The increased attention paid to industry standards is extending the importance of operational reusability. As standards mature and provide the foundation for greater portability between platforms, they will also be laying the foundation for wider reusability of system and design elements.

At present, the benefits of reusability depend directly upon the stability of the environment in which things are reused. A stable technical environment allows reuse of programs or program parts that control the environment for a variety of applications systems. A stable business environment allows re-use of specifications, requirements, and possibly a significant set of software when the technical environments change.

The stability under which reusability flourishes is becoming increasingly available as industry standards are being accepted and supported. This is particularly true for the operational environment.

As standards become more widely adopted, the boundary between reusable elements and system tools may be difficult to establish. Are the libraries in X-Windows development environments reusable software, or are they simply elements of the virtual machine?

Fourth-generation languages raise interesting questions about reusability. It may take less time to write a new 4GL program than to identify and incorporate existing, reusable program elements. In this case, is reusability worthwhile? Are we simply re-using high-level language constructs made possible by our data organization? Is it true that raising the level of abstraction at which programmers work will diminish the emphasis on reusability by making it transparent?

Questions such as these lead us from the issue of creating reusable software elements to the issue of reusability management. The management implications of reusability are far greater than, for example, the introduction of CASE. A software development organization that focuses on reuse of existing software and design elements is likely to be much different than the software development organizations of today.

There is a substantial break between the "clean sheet of paper" analysis and development methodologies we have grown up with and the "build upon what now exists" methodologies of an organization focused on reusability. The most lasting contribution of object-oriented methods to the computer industry may be the demonstration that effective reusability requires not just different tools, but a different way of thinking about the software process. This difference in methodologies becomes reflected in the redefinition of the development process management issues which must be addressed.

The heart of the reusability process management problem is the identification mechanism. How does one identify the existing system and design elements that are appropriate for re-use? Failure to identify suitable elements forces the development of new design and new code, undermining the goals of reusability.

The belief that identification problems can be solved at the code level is analogous to the belief that COBOL programs are self-documenting. Attempts to focus on reusability at this level are a key factor in the limited success of Ada and the SIGMA project. Reusability is an analytical consideration, not a programming consideration. For reusability to be effective, it is necessary to communicate clearly and effectively both the essence and characteristics of the elements which might be reused.

The key to reusability process management is that it must take place at the level of reusable design. Only at this level of abstraction will it be possible to supply analysts with the information which they will need to make reuse selections without extensive analysis of technical detail. The analysts themselves will need to be trained (or re-trained) to focus first on design classification, rather than beginning with new high-level abstractions and later refining them.

The continuing improvement in tools that generate application programs directly from design representations will aid the process of reuse substantially. The gains possible from this approach may be seen in the productivity improvements gained through the use of currently available application generators. One group within DuPont that makes extensive use of reusable design and application generators has been able to achieve and maintain a six-fold increase in development productivity[1].

To ensure that such gains become commonplace, development managers need to ensure that their analytical staffs are both knowledgeable and capable of developing design elements that are suitable for reuse. In addition, managers must ensure that their staffs have access to libraries of reusable design elements.

Libraries of reusable design elements might be supplied by CASE tool manufacturers. These companies have the most to gain from providing extensions that increase the value of their products. The presence of design

1. The majority of the group's work is in a limited applications domain.

libraries and the development of CASE interchange standards could provide the "critical mass" needed to shift the current software activity paradigm.

There is no question but that such a shift is overdue. Watts Humphrey's work on the software process[2] has shown how far we have to go. Despite years of arguments about the need to change programming from private art to public practice, there has been little movement away from the status quo. It seems clear that only the presence of financial benefits too substantial to overlook will be able to overcome the inertia of today's widespread software development inefficiencies.

The most substantial danger associated with attempts to change the development paradigm is the overstatement of benefits. Such overstatements have drastically slowed the acceptance of CASE, AI, and 4GL's and have poisoned the atmosphere for subsequent technical innovation. If we feed expectations that cannot be satisfied, we will do irreparable harm to attempts to promote reusability. The potential of reusability needs to be evaluated on a case-by-case basis and the limits of the possible must be established. The cost of adopting reusability must be established. The time and expense required to change the development paradigm must be clearly laid out.

It's interesting to reflect on the fact that one form of reusability has been so common as to almost escape notice in the Data Processing community. This form is data reusability. When we build new systems to replace old ones, or we change systems to do different things than they did yesterday, we assume that data that has been accumulated over time will continue to be used. One of the key points of this book is that organized and accessible data has led to process improvements and recurring benefits for the enterprise.

It might be useful to contemplate the reaction to an announcement by the Data Processing group that the new financial systems are ready to go, except that the company will need to discard all its current accounts receivable data. Most companies I have dealt with would regard this as a situation that deserved significant and immediate attention.

Anyone who has been part of a systems migration effort, whether from one set of computers to another, one operating system to another, or one applications system to another, knows that the care of the data is *the* critical task to be performed. The benefits of the new systems environment will never be enough to make up for a corrupted master customer file or lost records in the inventory data base.

2. Watts Humphrey's contributions have led to the "Process Maturity Model" used by the Software Engineering Institute. For further detail, read his book, *Managing the Software Process*, (Addison-Wesley, 1989).

One of the most promising aspects of the move to object based programming and analysis is the way that the reuse of data is incorporated with the reuse of processing elements. This alone may make the object based approach more successful than the previous "software library" approaches that dealt only with the process portion of the Data Processing task.

Even with the incorporation of both data and process, object-based elements are given value by the context in which they are used. Today's objects may lose some of their value if the context changes. Object based approaches can aid reusability, but they are no guarantee that development of original software will cease.

As the use of the object based approach to developing systems has spread, based on wider familiarity with the technique and additional tools, the Data Processing business appears to be finding that some of the old problems are still around. The objects used in constructing systems are objects that are specifically produced by the Data Processing organization to meet the specific needs of the enterprise. These objects embody assumptions about the business rules and processes that govern the practices that the systems support.

As object classes grow into the hundreds, understanding of the programming and analysis environment becomes more difficult to manage. Questions related to change management become more important as errors are found or enhancements to existing objects are created. Many of the characteristics of today's software maintenance environment are continued in organizations that have embraced object based techniques.

Adele Goldberg is known through her association with the *SMALL-TALK* object based environment, and is a leading spokesperson for object based techniques. She was quoted in a recent article: "Most people don't employ reuse; they do cloning." Cloning happens today as copies of existing systems are installed in new environments. The functional elements of the systems are not regarded or managed as individual resources. You get the whole cheeseburger or you get nothing—if you just wanted the bun, you have to bake a new one.

Furthermore, if you start out with reusable objects, there is no guarantee you'll finish up with reusable objects. Even in organizations which claim to have adopted object based technology and tools, changes are often made with no eye to the possibility of future modifications, or of use outside the application environment of the moment.

With the advent of integrated CASE tools that automatically produce code to be compiled and executed, the possibility of having reusable design elements has become more realistic. Some firms are beginning to create and sell templates of design elements, such as general ledger process designs that can be reused by any organization who needs to develop a new general ledger system. This approach has the advantage of raising the level of abstraction. It should allow the design elements to be analyzed and selected with less work than it takes to investigate large object classes. Still, the need to modify the selected designs will remain. The modifications will be made in order to meet the specific requirements of the task at hand.

We need to convince ourselves that reusability is not going to solve all our difficulties. Despite the fact that measurable gains are possible, reuse is not a silver bullet. There are limitations to reuse that come from outside the Data Processing environment. However, reuse can be a lead bullet, and even a lead bullet can be useful if one is trying to keep the wolves at a distance.

Too Much of a Good Thing

There are many Data Processing operations which remind me of my mother's attic. There's a lot of good stuff up in the attic. Some of it is stuff I put there because a) it was too good to throw out or b) I knew I was going to need it in a few months or c) stuff like that was a good thing to have around. My parents and sister put other stuff up in the attic for similar reasons. Heaven forbid that I should try to actually find anything up there. I also wonder if there might be some connection between all that stuff in the attic and some of the cracks in the bedroom ceiling.

Most of us have seen rooms full of big, fast disc storage units that spread out like some technologically advanced maze. But how many of us have asked the operations manager or Data Processing manager to provide a breakdown of the data that those discs contain? In all too many cases, the response is a look of concern and doubt, immediately followed by a disclaimer that the details could be easily obtained by the systems programmer.

In a number of situations where we have analyzed the contents of the discs, we found that a significant proportion of the data (over 80% in one case) was not regularly accessed by any production system.

There ought to be a law. Specifically, there ought to be a sunset law for systems and data. Sunset laws were originally proposed as a check on unnecessary government spending. It is obvious that legislatures preferred to spend time on making new laws rather than attending to those that are already on the books, and this has led to some strange situations. Perhaps the most notable was a law which existed in England. It required a man to stand on the cliffs of Dover with a telescope and sound a warning if he saw Napoleon coming. The job was abolished in 1948.

The purpose of Sunset Laws is to require each agency or program to justify its existence on a regular basis. If it could not do so, the agency or program was eliminated. The same principle should be applied to systems and data.

There is a lot of code and a lot of data on systems which simply isn't being used. It costs money to store this code and data. For one client, we were able to save over $250,000 per year by reducing the amount of data kept on line. With a smaller storage requirement, the client was able to reduce the number of disk drives and save on both lease and maintenance costs. In addition, he was able to put the plans for computer room expansion back on the shelf.

In looking at existing code for a system that generated invoices, we found that over thirty percent of the code was never accessed during execution. Changes had been made to the program to bypass existing code when new code was added but the existing code had never been removed. So-called "dead code" has a price that goes beyond the disk storage required. It can confuse programmers when they work on further changes to the program, raising the price of software maintenance and increasing the possibility of mistakes. In a very real sense the presence of program or data clutter makes efforts at reuse more difficult and expensive than they should be.

There can be waste even when the programs and data are relatively clean. We found several instances where weekly and monthly reports were being delivered to departments who sent them straight to recycling. Nobody looked at the reports because the information was either no longer relevant, or because it was available more conveniently through other reports or on-line access.

Why hadn't anyone noticed what was going on? The answer was that people had noticed it, but they felt that:

A. They didn't have the whole picture. If the Data Processing department was keeping this data or producing the reports, there must be some reason to do so.

B. It was more trouble to try to solve the problem than it was to ignore it. This was particularly true of programmers who put in the logic to bypass old code rather than to remove it. In some cases we found that the new code included much of the functionality of the code that was bypassed.

C. There wasn't any formal way of getting action to deal with the situation. Amazingly, we didn't find a single company with a formally documented procedure for removing a program from production. I'm sure this isn't universally true, but I'm surprised that I didn't encounter a single company that didn't follow the pattern.

A systems sunset law would set up a mechanism for sanity checks. People or departments who received reports would have to say that they still needed them. Data on the system would have to be sponsored in order to be retained. Programmers would have to provide convincing reasons for leaving dead code in place. These sanity checks might be done on an annual basis for reports and data, and more frequently for program code.

The benefits go beyond the savings associated with the amount of disk space and paper consumed. A systems sunset law also acts as a spur to make people think about the data that they are creating and using. It's an opportunity to take an introspective look at the way that systems are supporting business practices. It is an opportunity for improvement.

The mechanics of introducing a sunset law are fairly straightforward. Start by identifying each program, data file, or report, and determine a principal contact person. For programs this would be the Data Processing Manager or the programmer who is responsible for fixing problems and extending the program's functionality. For a report it is the person who receives it. For data files or databases it is a group made up of the people who use the data to support their business activities.

Pick an anniversary date for the program, file, database, or report. Sixty days before the anniversary, send out a notice to the primary contact and the heads of all business departments announcing your intention to remove the program, report, database, or files from the computer. Make sure you describe accurately what it is that you plan to remove.

Repeat the notice at the thirty day point. If you do not hear from anyone who needs the program or data, get on the telephone and spot-check some of the contacts you sent the announcement to. If nobody speaks up, get ready to remove the unused material from your production library or backing store.

Removing is not simply a case of deleting the files or programs. You should take the time to develop a formal procedure that includes a review of the operational aspects, including modification of any job control files. Make sure that the data or programs are backed up and that an accurate record of what has been removed is kept, both on the system and in an external log. Make sure that there is a plan for restoring everything if it is determined that it's needed. This is one of those things that shouldn't happen, but if you don't have a plan to deal with it, it will.

Once you have removed the programs and/or files, send out a follow-up notice telling everyone that you have removed them. You are not doing this to protect yourself, you are doing it to make sure that you haven't overlooked anyone who might be hurt when they no longer can find their program, or get a report that they use.

Reusability and control of your data and software base are two sides of the same coin. It may be tempting to keep large libraries of code and files with obscure or no-longer-used data because you will then have a larger set of things to reuse. Don't kid yourself. Trying to initiate a reusability program without first taking the time to ensure that your software quality justifies it is the same as developing a new-and-improved form of cancer.

Reusability and Funding Policy

Programmers and analysts like to create new systems. It's fun, it's challenging, it's creative, and it offers the opportunity to use new technical tools. Business executives like to get additional value from current physical plant and equipment, including their computers and software. A shift in the software paradigm from development to reuse offers a good opportunity to close some of the gap between the Data Processing organization and the general management of the enterprise.

Because reusability enables the software to provide a recurring benefit, it provides justification for classifying software itself as an asset. The asset can be valued. Investment in the asset to improve reusability can be advocated in a straightforward manner. Funds can be allocated to increase the value of the asset.

Many American businesses are at the point where their mission-critical systems must be replaced. Years of unplanned and under-managed changes to these systems have left them in a state where it is difficult to change or extend them. Data Processing managers are presenting estimates to corporate executives that show that thousands, even hundreds of thousands of dollars must be spent to re-engineer current software. Executives have not been slow to notice that most of this expense is going toward new programs and code which do the same things that current systems do.

If there is one thing that these men and women who have the final say on systems funding agree upon, it is that they do not want to be faced with another re-engineering scenario five or ten years from now. The only argument that has any credibility in responding to these concerns is that of reusability. The way to establish the needed credibility is to identify systems or parts of systems that can be reused now, or to show that the cost of changing current systems to make them reusable is less than the cost of developing new systems.

Ask yourself honestly if the systems you have today are so poor that it would be better to replace them in their entirety than to attempt to salvage parts that may still be of high quality. If you come to the conclusion that it's difficult to make that assessment, then you will have reached a point where you and your executive management are probably on the same wavelength.

17

Stupid

There's something very frightening going on in many companies today. It has many implications, few if any of them good. The worst part may be that we in the Data Processing business are helping to make it happen.

It's called "Dumbing Down" or "De-Skilling." It means reducing the skill content of a job so that it can be done by someone with less training and less intelligence. The enterprise saves on hiring costs, training costs, salaries, benefits, and the disruptions caused by people who care about their jobs and come up with ideas to improve things.

If the company is really committed to the "dumbing down" approach, it will achieve something it hadn't planned on. It will be a dumber company.

There are a lot of supposedly bright people working hard on ways to make companies dumber. Are you one of them? Are you sure?

The usual starting point to dumbing down a job is to treat it as part of a system. MacDonald's has a system for making french fries, and it turns out good french fries. However, the person who is cooking the french fries is not really "cooking" them. She's waiting for the alarm to give the proper number of beeps before she pulls the basket out of the fat. If she quits tomorrow, her replacement can be trained and ready to work in fifteen minutes.

If you think about what's happening, our french fry cook is no more than an attachment to the fry equipment. She checks the lights and listens for the buzzer. It really wouldn't be too difficult to have the whole process mechanized, but I suppose it would lose its human touch if that happened.

How far a jump is it from our french fry system with its "cook" to a loan officer at the bank who uses an expert system to help her decide if you are credit-worthy? Does the loan officer become, in reality, a data-entry clerk? Is she dealing with you at all, or are her customers just numbers on the screen?

The first banker I ever dealt with was my father's banker. Because he knew my father, he let me take out a ninety-day loan with no security. I did this twice before he retired. His successor wouldn't continue the practice, although I had a spotless payment record. The bank had adopted "new requirements." I no longer talked to the banker, I talked to the bank's new policy.

Perhaps our loan officer of today started out taking loan applications by phone. It's not difficult. Get the data, check the references, plug everything into a formula and see if the answer is "yes" or "no." All of this is done using a computer terminal and a telephone. As far as the bank's concerned, the only difference between selling money by phone and selling it at a desk is the dress code. After a few years of this, will our banker have accumulated any useful skills to help her career? What insights will she be able to contribute to the bank? How much personal involvement will she feel in loans that go sour if her expert system told her that the loan looked OK?

How do you feel about a bank that is directed by people who started out following directions on a terminal screen? Is it going to be an improvement over a bank that relied on human judgements about the character of the borrower? If you wouldn't trust your life savings to an expert system, would you trust them to an organization run by people who learned their trade by interpreting the outputs from expert systems? How much is this kind of bank going to contribute to the cities and towns we live in?

Over the past few years, we have been treated to a stream of bad news related to computers and financial institutions. When the Dow Jones average dropped by over 500 points in only a day, there were many people who pointed to program trading—a heavily automated procedure—as one of the root causes of the collapse. Subsequently, limitations have been announced to curb the extent of this type of trading. It remains to be seen how effective they will be.

The Savings and Loan debacle will haunt the American economy for years. While there is no doubt that venality played a significant role in this mess, there can also be little doubt that the people who both applied for and those who approved the shaky loans justified their actions through the use of involved spreadsheets that gave the "right" answer. After all, if it came out of the computer it had to be accurate.

The people who mistrust computers may not be as loony as they're sometimes portrayed. There is a dark side to the relationship between humans and computers, and it's not that computers will replace the humans. When a job is completely taken over by a machine, a human is free to go and do other things. This isn't always pleasant and it isn't always cheap, because re-training can be expensive. Still, using computers to completely eliminate human jobs may be better than the alternative.

All too often, computers are put to work in ways that discount human intelligence. It gives the people who must now use the computer less of a stake in their work, and less pride in it. It results in their thinking less about their work, and less about the welfare of the enterprise of which they are a part. We all know about jobs where people function as "organic peripherals" to computer systems. Would you want one of those jobs? Would you want your children to have one?

Dumbing down is not new, but it's picking up speed with computers. In many cases, the use of computers to get work done has the effect of discounting experience. The belief that: "If you can't measure it, you can't manage it" is taken as justification for ignoring relevant information which is difficult to quantify. It is this difficult-to-quantify information that is the product of experience in many cases. The expression: "If it looks too good to be true, it probably is" cannot be accommodated in a management or work environment that relies exclusively on quantifiable data.

We say we are in the information systems business. Information demands a certain degree of intelligence to give it value. How can we legitimately talk about building information systems that assume minimal intelligence in those who will use them?

Computers should do useful things for intelligent people, and they can. An expert system can help by organizing recorded experience which is relevant to a problem, and then assisting the user in reviewing the data. It should not be extended to tell the user what to do. The idea of an expert system that would automatically prescribe a course of treatment for a patient is anathema to competent physicians, many of whom see the potential of expert systems to assist them in diagnosis.

When you design a new system or make changes to an existing one, you can add significant value to your work by carefully thinking through the relationship between the system and its users. This is more than ergonomics. It involves an understanding of the nature of the work being done, including an understanding for its rewards, irritations, and potential for improvement.

Beware of the impetus to "improve" your system so that "users won't make so many mistakes" without first finding out more about what the mistakes are and why they're being made. If your car was delivered with square wheels, there are more useful ways of dealing with the problem than trying to improve the shock absorbers.

Computers are tools. We all know this, but we don't often think of the fact that while we use our tools, our tools, in subtle ways, also use us. The mental and physical tools with which we are familiar constrain our ability to view the world around us. Not only does the Lisp programmer look at problems differently than the COBOL programmer, he may not even be capable of seeing them the way the COBOL programmer does.

There is an on-going debate in academia and elsewhere concerning whether or not systems are truly intelligent. There are systems that "learn" from experience and we can expect their capabilities to get better as the future becomes the present. There is "fuzzy logic" which holds the promise of making some judgmental decisions manageable by machine. There are "smart systems" in industrial workplaces today with capabilities that would shock someone who was familiar with the industrial robotics of only ten years ago.

There is every reason to believe that a system could be built today which would satisfy the Turing test. In this test, a human operator communicates with another, unseen source of questions and responses. The test states that if the human cannot determine whether man or machine is the unseen correspondent, and if the correspondent is, in fact, a machine, then the machine is intelligent. The "Eliza" program developed over a decade ago was believed by many people to actually be a psychiatrist at the other end of the line. Even some psychiatrists believed it.

What are we to make of systems like these? How are we going to work with them? How will they affect our conception of who we are and what we do?

When we build systems, we are building tools, and we need to be conscious of our responsibilities to the people who will use them. If we insist on building systems that are aligned with minimal expectations about the abilities of the people who will use them, we will be undermining the value of our own work as well. As our users' work declines in value and our own work declines in value as well, the quality of all our lives will also decline.

And *that's* dumb!

18

PDU
Support

There is no clearer violation of Murphy's Law than the occurrence of a small serendipity. This is the story of a small serendipity and what became of it.

It was late in the morning and the ninety-minute presentation was going into its second hour. The meeting was to provide a project overview, but the project manager was having difficulty holding her audience back from dizzying plunges into low-level details. It was becoming yet another forgettable meeting.

The whiteboard was covered by lines and boxes—acronyms indicated existing and proposed systems. The project manager looked at the board and only half-heard a question about some hardware she knew nothing about.

She walked over to the board, looked for the red marker, and drew a huge circle around all the systems that were represented. Then she drew a little arrow at the top and, just above it, another box.

In the box, she wrote "PDU" in capital letters.

For a few seconds, there was silence. Then someone in the audience asked, "What's the PDU?"

"That," she said, "is the Poor Dumb User. He doesn't know how to discuss third normal form. He just knows simple stuff, like how to reorganize activity on the production line when the milling machine breaks. We are sitting here talking about how we are going to take $280,000 and build something that we will then ram down the throat of the Poor Dumb User. And we wonder why we're not appreciated. We have spent a little over two hours in this room and nobody, me included, has asked any questions about what all this means to the Poor Dumb User."

And that was the end of the meeting. But it wasn't the last anyone heard of the PDU.

The next week, the project manager prepared for another in the series of project presentations. She took her original chart and put it on the whiteboard, but reduced its size. Then she drew in the box labeled "PDU." It was much bigger this time.

This presentation was different. It ran a little longer than expected, but there was no problem controlling the level of discussion. For every feature of the proposed system, she bored in on the question, "So what's that mean for the Poor Dumb User?" This meeting turned up about six times as many action items as all the previous presentations combined because nobody on the technical staff was willing to say that he was really sure what the Poor Dumb Users needed.

This meeting led to something else that was unusual. The technical people went to work on the action items from the meeting by talking with the system users. But this time, instead of pushing the users for a sign-off on their latest system brilliancy, the systems people actually expected to listen carefully. And they did.

Although a couple of the details have been changed, this is a true story. The point hasn't come where everyone is living happily ever after, but things are getting better. "PDU Support" is becoming part of the folklore.

"PDU Support" sounds like an entry in the "gimmick of the week" contest. It isn't. The reason that it isn't is that the basic soundness of the idea is self-evident. The effect of setting up PDU support as a clear, publicly announced goal of the Data Processing organization is that it forces people to concentrate on what their work contributes, not just on what it is.

It's an easy goal to keep out in front of a technical organization. The technical executive can talk about PDU support at any time and in any forum. She can talk about it at meetings with the Poor Dumb Users themselves. She can set up methods of measuring the degree to which the PDUs are actually being supported, and she can demand performance improvements.

There's a lot of lip service going around about the way Data Processing is really a service group within the enterprise. It remains lip service until the question of "service to who?" gets a real answer. PDU support isn't real support until people on your staff sit down with flesh-and-blood Poor Dumb Users. It's not hard to make this happen. If you feel that someone on your staff is talking about PDU support as an abstraction, ask him for the name of the Poor Dumb User he's talking about. Don't forget that DP managers, too, have a responsibility to work one-on-one with some of the Poor Dumb Users they're supposed to be serving.

A Poor Dumb User can be a stock clerk or the president of the corporation. He can have twenty years of experience or twenty minutes worth. The Poor Dumb User is the one who is forced to figure out how he can use this system which was put together by all those geniuses in Data Processing. This does not make sense. If the geniuses are so smart, why can't they work with the Poor Dumb User to figure out what he needs and then deliver it? It doesn't even require geniuses.

I've never encountered a Poor Dumb User who took offense at the term. To most of them, it kind of summed up the frustration they felt after being treated as troglodytes by most of the Data Processing people they'd ever dealt with. The Poor Dumb Users know, with the certainty which comes from the truth, that if all the systems people disappeared there would still be a way to run the company. But if all the Poor Dumb Users disappeared, there would be no company to run.

The Poor Dumb User is a key to managing the value of the Information Asset. The value of your systems comes from the way in which they support business practices. The value of the Information Asset comes from the way that your Poor Dumb Users actually use the information. If you are supplying systems that force your users to work around *your* ideas in order to do *their* work, you are reducing the value of the data you are entrusted with managing.

When attempts are made to replace current systems, users often insist that certain features of the current interface be supported by the new system. The intensity of this insistence can be puzzling to systems designers who perceive opportunities to correct what they regard as idiosyncrasies in the current system. The truth of the matter is that users who have developed run-arounds to deal with system deficiencies are unwilling to trade advantages they have gained on their own for promises given by the systems development group.

Who can blame them? The fact that the Poor Dumb Users have found a way to make the system do what's needed is often the only sense of ownership they have in the system. This sense of ownership is important. Think of auto mechanics and their toolboxes, machinists and their lathes, and hardware technicians and their oscilloscopes. The pride in one's skills in using these tools is inextricably bonded to the sense of ownership of the tools. If we want our users to use the systems we build as effectively as possible, then these systems must be developed in a way that allows the Poor Dumb Users to establish ownership of what they do, and the way they do it.

A dialogue with Poor Dumb Users must be a true dialogue. The situation where the systems developers take every utterance of the user as gospel is as bad as the one where the developers treat the users as wayward children. Users will generally show a preference for the status quo and, without encouragement to change, this can cripple efforts to increase the value of the information asset. Developers, left to their own devices, may drift toward technologically interesting approaches that don't adequately account for the human element.

It is up to the developers to take the lead in talking to the Poor Dumb User at the level of the business practices that will be supported. At this level, both parties can consider the problems at hand without becoming mired in details. Furthermore, considering the underlying practices opens the door for substantial and far-reaching improvements in the business. Discussions of system details can't do this.

The key to any of this happening is for the systems people to take the initiative to develop meaningful ties to their users. It is likely to be slow going at first, as both sides will need time to learn to speak each other's language. Specific changes which are directly attributable to improved user/systems group communications may be hard to identify. Managers who are concerned about this should consider how difficult it is to determine how much credit the sun should receive when the corn crop is sold.

It's not hard to figure out how well your PDU Support program is going. Ask yourself the following questions:

- How many people who use my systems are on a first name basis with me? (We're talking about real users, not just their managers.)

- Outside of scheduled meetings, how often do I talk to my users about the system?

- How many of the complaints I hear about my systems do I personally follow through until resolution?

- How much time did I spend last week in places where my systems are being used? What did I learn that I didn't know before?

•When I come up with a great new idea for improving the system, do I bounce it off some users before I start discussing it with my own staff?

•When is the last time I publicly credited a user for contributions that improved one of my systems?

There's no point in cheating on this test. You probably already know your score.

So do your Poor Dumb Users.

19

The Right to Change One's Mindset

Changing the software development and maintenance paradigm to focus on information rather than data is an effort to change minds rather than an effort to change technology. The difficulty arises because of the way in which ways of thinking within the Data Processing profession are inevitably linked with the technology being used.

As Dijkstra observed, our tools not only change the way we think, they change our ability to think. Does this mean that the effort to change minds must be preceded by a change in technology? I don't think so.

The fundamental issue is to recognize that the programs and systems we produce are not ends in themselves. They are tools. Those of us who work to create systems seldom think of them that way. A payroll system is regarded as an object, a finished product, something that we built, something that stands on its own. We don't think of it as a tool that ensures people get paid in a timely manner. We don't think of it as a tool that provides data which can be used in labor negotiations. We don't think of it as a tool that influences corporate strategy.

The fact is that the payroll system is all of these things and more. We in the Data Processing arm of the enterprise don't regard it as a tool because we don't use it as a tool. Our tools are programming languages, operating systems, and file structures. Unlike the data we process, these are not shared by other parts of the organization.

Data Processing is a tool-making operation. Since our efforts deal with data, it's difficult for us to think of data in terms other than those that describe its physical and relational attributes. It is the recognition of what lies beyond things like field size and key definition that offers us the chance to begin changing the paradigm. As builders of tools, the extension of our activities to investigate the way in which the tools are used is a natural one. This is the most important element missing in the current way of doing things.

A company that manufactures socket wrenches has a sales force in the field. They observe how the tools are used, talk with customers about what they like and don't like, and think up ideas for new products and services related to socket wrenches. Many of these sales people use the socket wrenches in their own work, and they are able to talk to their customers using a base of shared experience. Data Processing doesn't have anyone who works this way. We exist in reactive mode, responding when users become frustrated to the point of raising their voices. Worse than that, we regard the people in our operations who deal directly with users as second-class citizens. Assignment to the Help Desk or to Problem Investigation and Repair is not generally regarded as a significant step up the organizational ladder.

Data Processing executives who emphasize the outputs of their organizations as tools rather than products are in a position to change the way Data Processing looks at itself. There are good reasons to do this.

The first is that it makes Data Processing work more rewarding for those who do it. All too often, the people who build systems never see them in action. They seldom see how their work has made a difference in someone else's life. This is a pity. The feeling of gratification that we get when we have worked in a productive team building a good system can be magnified by extending the team to include the people who will use the system. This is already a fact of life at the excellent DP organizations I have seen. It's possible to walk into a meeting where both DP staff and system users are present and have trouble distinguishing who works for Data Processing. Both system users and system builders share pride in the improvement of the overall work process, and this shows in the way they talk about what has been accomplished.

Some additional characteristics of these excellent organizations are worth notice. Productivity will be much higher than the norm in average Data Processing departments and turnover will be very low. When you talk to individual programmers and analysts, chances are good that they will want to show you their systems in action, letting you hear first-hand from the users about the quality and benefits.

A second reason to focus on systems as tools rather than as products is the way in which it spurs Data Processing to become a truly proactive function in the business. What develops is a constant and continuing interest in getting maximum value out of the systems and data used by the enterprise. By regarding systems as tools, the need to make them work together can be more easily seen and understood than if the systems were considered as products to serve specific needs. The linkage between the systems and the practices they support and enforce can only be clear if the systems are looked upon as tools.

The third, and most important, a view of systems as tools allows the Data Processing group and the enterprise as a whole to properly recognize the value of data as an asset that must be managed. The focus on processing rather than management of the underlying data has acted to obscure this issue in the Data Processing profession.

Once data is recognized as an asset, the funding process becomes more rational. The enterprise will be able to take a long-term view of investments in the information infrastructure and the tools that insure data accuracy and availability. On-going activities can be supported as well as short-term projects.

If the attempt to focus on data is made in an environment where systems are still considered products instead of tools, it is likely to become bogged down in discussions about technology issues rather than the information issues which are essential to the enterprise. Debates about centralized versus distributed file systems, or efforts to make the choice between hierarchical, relational, or object-oriented database technologies must not be based on technical merit only. Technical choices need to be considered in the context of the relationship between the data and the ways in which it is turned into information throughout the enterprise. Thinking about systems as tools can help establish this context.

Tools facilitate actions. In thinking about the data, if we understand the actions, we can choose the best tool accordingly. When we build a bookcase, we first think about the number and weight of books to be supported. Then we think about where the bookcase will be located. Then we think about what the bookcase should look like. We don't begin by checking to see if we have a box of two-inch screws.

It will not be easy to change twenty-five years of experience and an educational system which focuses on technology. Today our paradigm is focused on making systems run. We need to embrace a new paradigm that concentrates on assisting users to get the maximum information out of the data we manage. It is getting harder and harder to continue using the paradigm we have now. Redoubling our efforts and introducing new tools built on old assumptions will not be enough to allow Data Processing to live up to its potential.

In order for Data Processing to play the role it is capable of in the development of better, smarter, more personally rewarding enterprises the people in the Data Processing profession need to change the way they look at what they do and what they build. It's not necessary to throw out all that has gone before to make this change. It's not necessary to mount an attempt to change our technical environments. What's necessary is that we change direction and recognize that although we previously felt that the job of building systems was more important than understanding the way that data affected the enterprise, we now see the situation as reversed.

Data Processing people will continue to build systems. The systems will continue to accumulate, change, and distribute data. Users will continue to use this data to create information. The information will lead to actions by the enterprise that will, in turn, determine its success or decline. There's no magic here. It happens every day in hundreds of thousands of enterprises. By recognizing the continuity of the process and the role Data Processing plays in it, the information asset can be truly recognized as a key element of the foundation for the enterprise.

The End-Users

As Data Processing changes to regard its systems as tools that deliver data to users, it also needs to look at providing the users with better tools to use the data they receive. This is End-User Computing, where Data Processing's customers will manipulate data using tools of their own choice.

This is beginning to happen now. Reports are being transmitted to personal computers where users then import data into spreadsheets and organize, modify, combine, and display it in ways that help turn it into useful information. In this situation the end-users are relying on Data Processing to supply data, but not the detailed processing required to use it. The likely long-term effect on the Data Processing organization is the development of a split personality.

On one hand Data Processing will retain the responsibility for the development and care of the large-scale clerical and business systems used in the enterprise. Associated with that responsibility will be the task of stewardship of the information asset. This classic Data Processing activity will establish and maintain a foundation for an entrepreneurial environment, where specialized uses are made of the available data by people who have few formal ties to the Data Processing organization.

This entrepreneurial environment is populated by users and small teams who will be focused on opportunities to bring new products or services to market, or to improve the internal efficiency and responsiveness of the enterprise. In this environment there is a premium on speed and low cost. Most Data Processing groups are not organized to function optimally in this environment.

End-User Computing has typically been mistrusted by Data Processing organizations. It is seen as the source of support headaches —"Can you send someone over to help us configure our local area network?"—and of confusion and misunderstanding—"Those error rates don't match up with what I get out of my spreadsheets!" The reaction of Data Processing to End-User Computing can, at its worst, resemble a petty turf war.

The overwhelming majority of End-User Computing is designed to report data, not create it. It does not represent a threat to the integrity of data under the care of the Data Processing group. To be sure, end-users can make poor calculations and use invalid assumptions that yield misleading answers, but these problems are local and should have no systematic influence on business actions.

The growth of End-User Computing is one of the most powerful arguments for the enterprise to take an asset-based view of funding for Data Processing activities. Data Processing provides the platform that End-User Computing needs if it is to be effective. In advocating the asset based approach to funding, the Data Processing organization must clearly present its roles and responsibilities as they relate to End-User Computing.

The first of these roles is that of providing an accurate base of data and access to it. This has historically been the job of Data Processing and it is unlikely to be challenged.

The second role is that of being a tool provider to end users. In the sense of providing data, this role is already being performed. In another sense, that of providing assistance to the end users in the selection and implementation of End-User Computing tools, Data Processing has been content so far to let users make their own choices. This is a mistake.

In order to be truly effective, end users need something more than the latest spreadsheet or graphing package. They need better tools to find and organize the data they put into their matrices and graphs. Data Processing has been content to build systems that deliver data. There has been little effort to develop and deliver data access tools.

One reason for this is that Data Processing programmers and analysts themselves often have difficulty in finding and obtaining access to the data that they need to develop or modify the systems they are responsible for. The idea that end users would want to do this, or that they be allowed to roam through the data in the way that Data Processing staff do, is simply unthinkable.

The idea that tools should be developed that ease the task of locating and accessing needed data has not yet taken hold. Data Processing should make this a priority task. Data Processing's active support of End-User Computing has the potential to dramatically increase the value of the information asset.

Historically, dramatic increases in the value of computing have come from end user involvement. From the business people who went to IBM classes to learn how to program the IBM 1401 in Autocoder™ to the managers who obtained a copy of Visicalc™ or Lotus 1-2-3™ for their personal computers, end users are the ones who have been the pioneers in finding new ways to use computers and data to support business activities.

By encouraging end-users by developing tools that locate and extract data from today's complex databases, Data Processing is investing in its own future. Increases in Data Processing's value to the enterprise will be based on the degree to which end-users incorporate computer-managed data into their daily work. Graphic interfaces, fuzzy logic, and artificial intelligence may all have some role to play in the development of intelligent browser software that can be adapted by end users to get at the data they need.

"Groupware" and electronic mail systems allow the end users to work in collaboration without direct involvement by the Data Processing organization. As end users extract and manipulate data and exchange it with one another, Data Processing becomes regarded less as a bottleneck and more as a facilitator.

Data Processing will, over time, change its emphasis from systems that deliver data to a two-pronged approach:

•It will concentrate on the infrastructure that supports the asset. This includes the clerical systems that gather and organize large volumes of original data used by the enterprise. It also includes investment in the improvement of data quality and access mechanisms.

•It will develop and deliver tools that allow end users to locate and access data for further manipulation. Not only should these tools include the means for end users to share information, but they must also provide safeguards to ensure confidentiality of sensitive data.

The development and management of a second culture (the tool builders) within Data Processing organizations will cause institutional strain. The technologies and operating practices of the two groups will probably differ, and each will use terminology and work practices that are related to the technical environment in which they work. Current job classifications will become inadequate.

Many enterprises will place the different functions in independent organizations. This is the easy way to proceed. It is also the wrong way. The effectiveness of the tool builders will depend in large part on the resources provided by those who manage the large-scale systems and data. In turn, the value of the large-scale systems and data is extended by the products of the tool builders. Coordination of the activities in both areas of Data Processing is necessary to reap the full advantage possible with increased capabilities for end-user computing.

This coordination involves more than different areas of Data Processing. It must be extended to include the end users as well. There needs to be a recognition that the days are past when the users "signed off" on systems requirements and all subsequent communication took place through Software Change Request Forms. Moving the Data Processing orientation from one of delivery of data to one of delivery of tools means that the Data Processing staff must become proactive in their dealings with end users.

The Data Processing organization will be constantly offering end users improved tools for data access and processing. Support will move toward training and tutoring instead of documenting and delivering. Only by working closely with the end users will it be possible to understand the ways in which current tools are used and to recognize the possibilities for improvement.

It may seem like a roundabout route, but the increasing presence of End-User Computing may be the catalyst to bring Data Processing and those it serves closer together than they are today.

20

Moving Toward a New Information Culture

The promise of an information economy is in the air. The joining of computing, telecommunications, and image processing is seen as opening the door to a new world of work and leisure. Even Timothy Leary, who previously advocated an approach of "Tune in, turn on, drop out" is now holding forth "virtual reality" as the key to the culture of the future.

Many enterprises are looking hard at Data Processing as an area that is critical in turning information into strategic advantage, so they will be prepared for the information economy. "Strategic Process Re-Engineering," "Rightsizing," and a number of other initiatives are embraced because of the promise that they will unlock corporate creativity and control spiralling costs—all this while leading to a corporate culture characterized by quality and excellence.

In some cases the promises will be kept. Dramatic improvements will happen. Companies will emerge as the subjects for future "best practice" studies, taking their places alongside the best practice companies that they studied on the road to improvement.

In other cases good intentions will not be matched by equally good results. In many of these instances the pressure to keep pace with today's activities will leave too little time and too few resources for the investment needed to insure long-lasting changes. The price of doing things differently and the projected length of time before the new ways of business are expected to show dividends will conspire to preserve the status quo. People who might champion the needed changes will hold back. After years of running things while looking at the short-term view, many managers will find it difficult to accept the risks associated with a longer-term approach.

Despite these conditions, the forces for change are moving forward. The leading edge companies who have found ways to take advantage of their information assets are generating market forces that threaten the survival of companies unable to keep pace. Wal-Mart, Banc One, and Federal Express have all raised the expectations of customers and, in turn, they have put pressure on their competitors' business processes. On a larger scale, the government of Singapore and Telecom France are implementing changes to their national infrastructures based on strategies that call for improved use of information assets.

The handwriting is on the wall, although the letters are still faint. The business of building and maintaining Data Processing systems cannot continue for the next twenty years in the same way it has for the past twenty.

The focus of Data Processing must move from technical minutiae to process outcomes. Technology is not the problem. Our enterprises have never lacked the ability to throw technology at problems. We didn't get to the point we are today through lack of technology investment. Despite this, the knee-jerk reaction to the challenges of an information economy is to look for new technology. Do we really think that client-server or object-oriented or ___(your choice of "breakthroughs" here)___ is the answer to all our problems? How long are we going to go on kidding ourselves?

According to Alfred French in *The Business Knowledge Investment*, "Proof of information divergence is seen increasingly as each new round of technology recreates what already exists rather than building a standard foundation for expansion. Little attention is given to shifting mental gears: Only new, faster engines are perceived."[1]

If we come to the point where the roles of information and Data Processing are re-cast within the enterprise, it will probably be the result of a

---

1. J. Alfred French, *The Business Knowledge Investment*, (Prentice Hall, 1990).

difficult on-the-job journey. We will begin that journey with the data and systems we have now, and we will carry them with us for a good while.

Many strategically important systems today are old enough to vote. They have grown from modest beginnings to encompass a wide range of functionality. They have evolved to handle conditions unique to the environments where they are used. In some cases these systems, that at first were a contributor to the growth and prosperity of the enterprise, now function as straightjackets preventing change and expansion.

A study performed by Sasa Dekleva of DePaul University and published by Software Maintenance News in February, 1991, showed that the typical software system of 1980 had 23,000 lines of code and 55 programs. The typical software system of 1990 has 1,246,000 lines of code and 589 programs. Most of 1990's typical systems are being written and maintained using 1980 methodologies, 1980 programming languages, and 1980 management approaches.

Wholesale replacement of these systems is not a viable business proposition. The cost for building new, large systems is high, and is likely to be considerably higher than the initial estimates. Considering the percentage of large systems development projects that are never completed, the true cost of a replacement effort is likely to be well in excess of the cost of the system to be replaced.

The value of the information kept in computers becomes highly visible when large systems that have been developed over many years are actually replaced. The effect of system replacement can be similar to the after-effects of a fire. The flow of information becomes interrupted. People are forced to change the way they work. Mistakes occur which jeopardize relationships with customers and suppliers.

Still, when the level of competitive pain or legislative pressure mandates that the systems be replaced, the enterprise will find a way to do it.

System replacement projects based on in-house development of new software frequently have long-term impacts because of the way in which they dilute the systems expertise of the enterprise. Technical staff knowledgeable in both the current system and its business applications must be assigned to develop the new system, but they will inevitably be called back to work on the current system when it encounters trouble. With the maintenance and enhancement backlogs typical of most Data Processing environments, there is seldom sufficient time to train replacements to fill in for the in-house experts when they are assigned to other activities. The consequence of all this is that any attempt to use in-house expertise in developing new systems often results in making the maintenance and enhancement backlog worse. It's a vicious cycle that usually winds up burning both people and money.

Incremental re-engineering is an obvious alternative to massive development projects or other forms of wholesale systems replacement. The move toward re-engineering is an initiative to remove the constraints of current systems through the normal process of enhancement activity. Today's systems will be analyzed, broken apart, and reassembled in a manner that will remove the current limitations—or, at least, that's what's supposed to happen.

In practice re-engineering has been a difficult undertaking. The difficulty starts with the task of documenting the systems currently in place. The reverse engineering of current systems is primarily a manual effort today, with limited tools available for automating the task of analyzing existing system process logic (or illogic). Although there are several instances where the analysis and documentation tasks have provided short-term payback,[2] it's very difficult to quantify either cost or payback at the beginning of the analysis effort.

Once the analysis of the current system has been completed, Data Processing attempts to organize what has been learned and what is known of the business needs into a set of software resources that can be combined to yield a better system than the one currently in place. Again, this is not an easy task. It has been likened to peeling the layers from an onion and then reassembling it. Many tears are shed as the work moves forward.   As Tom DeMarco so accurately put it: "The truth will set you free, but before it does it will make you miserable."

It is at this point in the process that the object-oriented techniques may turn out to be particularly valuable. By formally joining the data elements that must be preserved to the process elements that provide access to them, the current system can be segmented in a manner that has clear ties to the business processes it supports. This may allow the Data Processing staff to better communicate the role and functionality of a system to the business process managers who are the system's real users.

This communication is the point when we can begin to move away from today and into the future.

Long-term advantage comes from improvements in fundamental processes, not from the momentary advantages which are the outputs from those

---

2. Aetna Insurance saved almost 50% in maintenance costs over three years through staff reduction following a reverse engineering documentation project. The volume of maintenance activity was not reduced.

processes. I'm not aware of any features that you can order with a Toyota that you can't also order with a Ford, but Ford representatives have been very forthright when they describe Toyota as their competition because of the quality of Toyota vehicles. The quality comes from the accumulated improvements in Toyota's manufacturing process over the years. It is virtually impossible for competitors to make up disparities in fundamental process competencies through crash programs or the like.

The key to keeping up with the competition is organizational learning: Not just the learning of new facts and production techniques, but learning how to improve the organization's ability to learn.[3] The pacesetting companies of today all place great value on organizational learning. They talk about it, they think about it, and they try to measure it. They look at Kaizen, the Japanese practice of on-going incremental improvement. They look at Cypress Semiconductor, which attempts to apply its organizational learning through "killer software" that enforces business policies.

In examining today's leading enterprises, two themes become clear. First, that the overwhelming majority of these companies started without a significant material advantage over their competition. They took what they had and did a better job of improving themselves than their competition did. Second, they improved by keeping their eye on the entire enterprise, learning how to make all the parts work better together.

Organizational learning starts by taking a new look at what your enterprise knows about itself: its processes, its customers, its competition, its quality, its strengths, and its weaknesses. In taking that look the enterprise also needs to identify what it should know but does not. All of this ties back to the data that the corporation keeps.

The task of taking this new look must be a cooperative one, with business and Data Processing personnel working closely together. Just as the managers of the enterprise are told to improve their understanding of their business by getting closer to the customer, Data Processing also needs to get closer to its customers—the business process managers. Without an active partnership with the business managers, the Data Processing managers will not be able to understand the strengths and deficiencies of the process they manage. They will be unable to improve Data Processing for the benefit of the enterprise.

What should Data Processing organizations learn? First, they should learn how their products are used. This, in turn, means that they must learn to

---

3. Arie de Geus has stated that the ability to learn is the only sustainable strategic advantage.

speak the language of their users. As they change their way of talking about what their systems do, programmers and analysts will become more business-problem oriented because they will be spending more of their time working with system elements defined at the business function level. The proportion of time and effort spent on solving technical problems will go down. We can see the potential of this manner of work today in a few very effective Data Processing organizations, such as those in the United Services Automobile Association (commonly known as USAA) and the British Columbia Telephone company.

Second, Data Processing organizations must learn about their own processes by taking the time to measure them and study them. Today, it's all too common to discover that systems "just happen." The research performed by the Software Engineering Institute shows that the majority of enterprises examined have software processes which are classified as "chaotic."

The Process Maturity Model used by the Software Engineering Institute[4] and the System Dynamics Model developed by Abdel-Hamid and Madnick[5] provide frameworks for Data Processing organizations who wish to look analytically at the way they do business. Data Processing organizations who are making a serious attempt to become smarter about the way they work will be aware of these models, and will try to build effective models for their own process.

The important work of evaluating the current state of the enterprise's systems and business processes is not high-tech work. It requires time and dedication, both of which are often in short supply. It also requires the formation and growth of a community of interest within the enterprise.

This community of interest needs to include the managers with line responsibility for getting things changed. Although it is helpful to have the backing of senior management, their presence is not enough to assure success. The world is full of executive decrees, vision and mission statements, and high-level task force reports of every description. I recently served on a very high level study project that almost came to a halt when a senior vice-president in the firm said: "This all looks very good, but what's the difference between your study and the last one?"

There may not have been much difference. Many organizations have known for years that they needed to improve Data Processing and the way information was used in the enterprise. Suggestions related to data consoli-

4. Watts Humphrey, *Managing the Software Process*
5. Tarek Abdel-Hamid and Stuart E. Madnick, *Software Project Dynamics: An Integrated Approach*, (Prentice Hall, 1991).

dation and data quality aren't necessarily original because this is the first time that *we* thought of them.

When we begin to look for a community of interest that is concerned about improving the processes of the enterprise and achieving long-term advantages, we may find that the most difficult concept to sell is that this time, things can be changed. In a lot of organizations the sweeping changes announced in previous years have produced more cynicism than results.

Change can be brought about by focusing on how Data Processing decisions are made, and not on the results which follow those decisions. Previous initiatives— "We are going to standardize on Open Systems!"—may carry the ring of conviction, but they remain divorced from day-to-day activities. An announcement that: "We are going to get as many of you as we can to help us make the decision whether or not to standardize on open systems" hits closer to home. It looks at a process in terms of its outcomes, not only for the open systems decision, but also from the standpoint of establishing commitment and building understanding.

The work of improving the process takes longer since it's an effort to change people and not just technology. The saving grace is that it takes the longest the first time. Subsequent shifts in Data Processing and information use can be made in an atmosphere where people are more comfortable with change. The organizational learning that is so important will have begun.

Thomas Kuhn, in his classic book, *The Structure of Scientific Revolutions*[6], writes about the inertia and resistance that greet each new paradigm of scientific thought. In Data Processing, the task of change is even more difficult. No clearly defined paradigm exists that unifies the relationship of the high cost, misunderstood specifications, and on-going maintenance demands of today's data processing environment to the business processes and organizational protocols that Data Processing must support.

By concentrating on the process of change rather than the end result, Data Processing will be drawn to look more closely at ways in which the current information assets can be leveraged to provide additional value to the enterprise. The line of demarcation between support and development will be erased as the focus on process improvement becomes the normal mode of operation. This change will benefit the enterprise in several ways:

•It provides added recognition for work that supports day-to-day operations. Today, this work often takes a back seat to the development of new systems that use the latest tools or techniques.

6. Thomas A.Kuhn, *The Structure of Scientific Revolutions*, (Van Nostrand Reinhold, 1961).

•It provides a better career path for technical staff who possess valuable systems/business knowledge. It allows them to build on that knowledge and raise their value to the enterprise. There is no need for them to escape from maintenance and enhancement activity in an attempt to get a share of the development spotlight.

•The training of new technical staff receives closer supervision and support. There is no artificial rush on behalf of experienced technical staff members to "find a warm body to fill this slot so that I can go do development."

As business knowledge is brought into the Data Processing organization, the level of abstraction at which work is performed will rise. This makes issues of coordination between systems and multiple business processes easier to handle.

The longest-lasting effect of this new way of building systems will be the effect on the people who build them. The history of Data Processing so far has concentrated on the ability of programmers and analysts to accommodate technical constraints. These constraints were imposed by the computers, networks, and terminals that made up the physical computer system. As a result of breakthroughs in the price and performance of component electronics and the development of software-generating tools that allow the programmer to think about the problem, the need for in-depth technical knowledge will be reduced.

The important thing to keep in mind is that the forces driving the changes in the Data Processing culture are not something that can be managed by fine tuning the way systems are built today. Our current ways of building systems have left us with systems that can no longer keep up with business needs. The complexity, cost, and difficulty associated with building replacements for these systems cannot be managed by following the same practices that brought us to where we are now.

As organizations become more reliant on information flows provided by computers, they will find themselves increasingly backed into a corner as the constraints of their current systems become more noticeable. If these organizations recoil from the level of investment in both money and time that will be required to change the Data Processing culture, they will be putting their survival at risk. Although this might sound over-dramatic, it is quite realistic. Competitors who are better able to adapt their systems to accommodate changes forced by regulation, competition, and market requirements will be able to operate at lower cost and respond more quickly to opportunities. If a competitor is able to match your quality and service for a cost fifteen percent below yours, you will have trouble maintaining any market share over the long term.

In the end, changing the Data Processing culture is not a technical choice—it's a business choice. Until Data Processing learns to think of its activities in business terms, as caretakers of the information asset, it will not be able to exert effective influence on the process by which systems are funded, built, and used.

Index